brief intervals of horrible sanity

remy

P.

Tarcher /Putnam

a

member

of

Penguin

Group

(U.S.A.)

Inc.

New

York

one season in a

brief
ef

int
erv
als

of

progressive school

hor
rib
le

sa
nit
y

eli
za
be
th

go
ld

Most Tarcher/Putnam books are available at special quantity discounts for bulk purchase for sales promotions, premiums, fund-raising, and educational needs. Special books or book excerpts also can be created to fit specific needs. For details, write Penguin Group (U.S.A.) Inc. Special Markets, 375 Hudson Street, New York, NY 10014.

Although the events described in this book are true, I have changed the name of the school and the names of all the members of the faculty and the students to protect their privacy. I have also imagined what some of my students might well have thought, felt, written, and said in instances where I wasn't present or where they didn't actually express their thoughts and feelings to me. Furthermore, while the incident involving "Sarah" did really happen, the actual texts of the letters were also imagined.

Jeremy P. Tarcher/Putnam
a member of
Penguin Group (U.S.A.) Inc.
375 Hudson Street
New York, NY 10014
www.penguin.com

Library of Congress Cataloging-in-Publication Data

Gold, Elizabeth, date.
Brief intervals of horrible sanity : one season in a progressive school / Elizabeth Gold.
p.   cm.
ISBN 1-58542-244-4
1. Children with social disabilities—Education (Secondary)—New York (State)—Jackson Heights (New York)   2. Education, Secondary—New York (State)—Jackson Heights (New York)   3. High school teaching—New York (State)—Jackson Heights (New York).
I. Title.
LC4093.J33G65      2003                    2003040279
373.747'1—dc21

Printed in the United States of America
1   3   5   7   9   10   8   6   4   2

This book is printed on acid-free paper. ∞

Book design by Stephanie Huntwork

To the teachers of the School of the New Millenium,
who taught me the true meaning of grace under pressure.

I became insane, with long intervals of horrible sanity.
edgar allan poe

I'm no expert.

If you open this book expecting to learn about everything that's wrong with the schools today and the surefire solution, you're going to be disappointed.

I'm no angel, either.

It seems stupid to state the obvious, but I feel like I must. Somehow, these days, to admit you're a teacher without a halo and wings is to admit you're nothing less than a monster.

I'm not a monster. At least, I don't think I am. Though there were certainly times at the School of the New Millennium when I felt like one.

Say, instead, I am simply a human being who got herself in over her head.

Why do I feel I have to insist on this?

Could it be because I have just recently left that Manichean battleground of left, right, good, bad, that is School?

It could.

In the year 2000, education, as an issue, was in the air.

In one way or another, for the past one hundred years, anyway, it has always been. Scroll through your average library catalogue and read the titles about *What's Wrong and How to Fix It* and *Making the Classroom Fit the Child*. Then read the year the last one was published: 1924.

But as the twenty-first century was beginning, things suddenly felt more urgent. Perhaps we were living in a new era—The Information Age—an era, if you were going to thrive in it, that required all kinds of knowledge and new skills—but forget advanced knowledge: many of our students could barely read, write, do math. About twenty percent of New York City students dropped out of high school. Of the remaining students, only half managed to graduate in four years. And when new standardized reading tests were instituted in 1999—tests that actually required students to read and respond to text, as opposed to simply answering multiple-choice questions—it was revealed that only 35.3 percent of the students were reading at grade level or above.

In other words, while politicians were intoning the motto of the day, *We will leave no child behind,* the evidence was in: we were leaving quite a few behind. And in case you think this was only a New York City problem, it's not: in Rochester, Yonkers, Syracuse, Buffalo, and other New York State cities, the passing rate was only 26.8 percent. And examples of such unnerving statistics can be found all over the country.

Which is where I come in.

When I became a ninth-grade teacher at the School of the New Millennium in Jackson Heights, Queens, I planned on doing a good job. But I didn't plan—in the end refused—to do what somehow I ended up feeling I was supposed to do—embrace a life of noble self-sacrifice, spend my days thinking of nothing but how I was going to *reach* those kids. I like reading books, I had had a variety of teaching experiences, I enjoyed—or thought I did— being in front of the classroom. None of that seemed to matter when I began my stint in this slightly peculiar public school.

It is often said that education reform goes in pendulum

swings. And this is true. Some event occurs—say, the launching of Sputnik into space—and politicians and academics and journalists suddenly notice a problem that has been going on for years. They then start clamoring for solutions—choosing to forget, or not bothering to notice, that whatever school philosophy is current, it is usually something that was once guaranteed as a solution for the solution that had been guaranteed before.

I began working at the School of the New Millennium at a peculiar wobble of the pendulum swing. Many students had started school when the concept of self-esteem was big. Students didn't do well, it was believed, because they felt bad about themselves. If they felt better, they would excel. Textbooks were written and teaching methods developed out of this philosophy. But now things were changing. The latest fashions were now Standards, and the tool that was supposed to make standards happen—standardized testing.

The minute you start talking tests, you must consider that the point of a test is that some people pass, and some fail. Thus making them feel bad. You would think that one philosophy would cancel the other out, but, at least at the School of the New Millennium, that's not what happened. Both philosophies were promoted at exactly the same time. No wonder my students were confused. I was, too.

I still am. But maybe that's the point. Once I entered the School of the New Millennium, I lost the luxury of distance. Maybe I, too, once dreamed an ideal dream of what people were supposed to be, and how, through the simple force of my goodwill, I could reach them. Now I know it's far more complicated than that.

so, class, shall we begin?

"This is why Columbine happened."

Cindy Fernandez, on the other side of the room, is yelling something. She's got a loud voice, a voice part bullhorn and part plaintive baby, and when she decides to use it, which she does, often, there's not much space for anything else. She's yelling something, something insulting, which again, is something she does, often, and the only thing I notice, as I huddle in my chair, as close to Peter Garcia as I can manage without being obvious about it, is that she's not, for a change, insulting *me*. Why should I care, why should I be such an egomaniac to mind what anyone says to me, but yet I notice its absence, the absence of insult of me, I can, instead of being the target, watch this: Cindy Fernandez whip up the two girls on either side of her, her cronies, two-thirds of class 9B's very own Witches of Endor, Cindy Fernandez whip them up, and thus her side of the room, into a passion. A passion of what? It doesn't matter: a passion of passion. The thing itself, a motor simply whirring with no purpose but the whir.

Peter Garcia pushes his chair back, which is a sign that he is pissed off, really, *Say any more, Cindy Fernandez, and you might be sorry,* because while Peter is no macho posturer, and certainly, no bully, he is a *Hobbit*-reading, skateboarding, peace-loving boy, he has a sense of honor and self-respect that many an adult might envy and "This," he repeats, in that calm voice of his, that voice that never loses its cool, *"this* is why Columbine happened."

I agree. I agree. I have begun to understand, from the inside now, how high school can be a place of such storm and terror that something terrible could bubble up in a boy. How day after day of insult and confusion and the thought that this is it, that these classmates, these halls, are the world, the only world, could corrode you from the inside out. I think this, and worst of all, it doesn't even shock me to think this. It is late in the year, and I have about given up the policing which, despite any high-falutin' language to the contrary, I was really hired to do: *Hats off, do-rags off, Walkmans off, hands off, Tim, did you hear me? Save it for later. Save it for the park. The street. The gutter. Shirts on. Pants on. Is that all you're wearing, Miss? Big Macs put away. French fries put away. Sodas put away. Magazines put away. Is that the language you want to be using? Hats off. Do-rags off.* And so on, and so on. I have given it up, I almost never even walk to the other side of the room, the side of the room ruled by Cindy Fernandez instead of Peter Garcia.

"Yeah," says Peter, "it started like this," and before I can stop myself, I talk to him the way I would to anybody, I am so grateful to have that sane human presence in the room that I quite forget he is just fifteen. "I'll say," I snap. "I'm surprised a teacher didn't grab a machine gun and do it *herself*."


I appall myself.

How could I have said such a thing, such a heartless thing?

I appall myself.

But now I have the luxury of appalling myself. I am not in that room, that room I grew to hate, Room 313, with its computer screens and its sour human smell and the one window too high up and too small for anyone to jump out of. I'm not in that room, if I have any luck at all I'll never walk into that damn room again.

This is a story about high school. But not only a story about high school. It may be more accurate to say this is a story of idealism run amok, in a place that happens to be a high school.

In some ways it could be any high school. There are bullies and the bullied; long dull days and moments of enlightenment; virtuoso teachers and those who need a course or two in classroom management. There's a principal intoning the improving jargon of the day and posters on the walls telling those who can't read to *Read!* as if that word alone should do it.

There are students planning their escape, and students, God help them, for whom this will be the best moment in their lives.

So yes, the School of the New Millennium in some ways can be any school. But it has its own particular story. It's a big-city high school, for one, a multiethnic school in the middle of an immigrant middle-class and working-class neighborhood. Furthermore, the School of the New Millennium was—and I guess, still is—a high school with a mission. The goal of this school is not simply to graduate students but to transform them. Into the loving, compassionate Leaders of Tomorrow. Building Our Future New York, Soul by Caring Soul, Today.

A worthy goal, I suppose.

Not that I ever figured out how to do it. Though I did suspect—I really did—that cowering behind my desk was not the way.


So I'm not perfect teacher material. I guess it's not that surprising. I don't have a Ph.D. in education. I don't even have a permanent teaching certificate. When I entered the School of the New Millennium, I had never even taught high school before. But in some ways, at least on paper, I look great.

First of all, unlike the gym coach suddenly transformed into the science teacher, I not only *knew* my subject—English—but loved it. I'm a poet, and have been published in some pretty good journals. I'm also a compulsive reader, always have been. And while it is true I had no prior high-school teaching experience, I had taught in plenty of other places before, and had had some success, perhaps even changed a life or two. Ask my students at the branches of City University I taught in. They'll tell you the same. I had taught younger kids, too. I had traveled around the city as a writer in the schools. Do you know what a high it is to walk into a classroom to hear thirty or so ecstatic eight-year-olds screaming, "She's here! The poet!"?

Is that what I thought would happen to me at the School of the New Millennium? Did I think I would suddenly become one of those cool teachers with really good cheekbones and a nice leather jacket who would get *through* to the kids no one had gotten through to before? Had I seen one too many movies? Did I imagine surging violins?

*Uh* . . .

Well. I *had* read the School of the New Millennium brochure. It sounded great. Maybe I can be forgiven for thinking that. A New Visions school . . . why not? A lot of the old ones didn't work very well.

When the New Visions for Public Schools, a nonprofit organization, was founded in 1989, it was responding to a reality, and a pretty ugly one at that. It's not that the New York City public school system was failing everybody. It was possible then, as it is now, to get a good, even a great education in the city schools. If you tested into the right ones. If you had family support and backing. If you ran into one of those genius schoolteachers scattered throughout the system who would recognize your particular gifts and find a way to develop them. Or if you were so focused you were going to thrive no matter what your circumstances. So it's not that everybody was failing. It's just that a lot of people were failing a lot.

Those statistics I quoted earlier are tricky, as statistics often are. For yes, there is a 20 percent dropout rate; half of the remaining students graduate in more than four years, and of course, there are those horrendous reading scores. But what that actually means is, is that in some schools, almost nobody dropped out. Almost everybody graduated on time, and was working at grade level or above. In other schools, it was mixed. And in other schools, it was failure. The real chaotic deal.

It was that disparity that New Visions for Public Schools tried to address. The concept behind it and other organizations started around that time was, *If education as we know it isn't working, let's try something else.* While its proposed solutions were myriad, the one fundamental belief that it tried to promote was *small is beautiful.* In a small school, students and teachers get to know each other, work together, and love each other like a family. In a small school, kids don't get lost, and nobody gets left behind.

In 1992, the then chancellor of the New York City Board of Education, Rudy Crew, asked New Visions to come up with new designs for schools that would put some of its theories into action. So it did. The School of the New Millennium was one of them.

Look, I'm not going to talk about what has happened, and is happening, in the other schools. Maybe they are very successful. It would be nice to believe they are. But even though I've read a few articles, what my experience in my classroom has taught me is that a journalist sitting in the back of the room sees only part of the picture, so I can't tell you what those schools are really like. Each school has its own culture and chemistry. You have to live it to know it. I'm not going to make a generalization about all those other schools. I can't.

This is what I know. The School of the New Millennium is a school with a mission. I'm not opposed to missions, though maybe I'm not the kind of person to go on one. I'm too allergic to slogans, too loyal to the opposite point of view. But I will say this: at least some people noticed something was wrong. At least they tried. And if the mission at times got, well, kind of out of hand, is that so surprising? Missions are difficult. Missions can explode or implode as easily as stars.

But as to how that happens, or if they can somehow manage to put themselves, against all the laws of astrophysics, together again, now there's the tale. So. Did I ever get out from behind my desk? Square my shoulders, find my courage, thanks Peter Garcia but *I'm taking over now, kid,* and finally I *do* get through to them, have them ace the chess match/cheerleading trials/citywide math exam, and next thing you know, they're yodeling a song in my name? Did I ever lose those five pounds, grow two inches, pull the citywide dropout rate down to 10 percent, and the nationwide performance on standardized science tests above, say, Slovenia's? And most of all, did I, after much morally improving struggle, learn something deep and revealing about myself, increase *everybody's* self-esteem—yes, that includes my own—and, as I had been instructed to do, finally come to love all the children, equally? This, as they say in the school yard, is for me to know, and you to find out.

february
**a leader of today**

# The New Millennium is here . . .
# and we're meeting the challenge.

*Welcome to the School of the New Millennium*
*Developing New York's leaders of the future . . . today.*

## OUR HISTORY . . .

**In** April 1992, the NYC Board of Education asked New York citizens to submit ideas for creating several "New Visions Schools." Fifteen teachers and parents met to plan such a school. Concerned about the future of New York, the group wanted to create a school that would help improve life in the city . . . that would develop informed, sensitive, humanistic young leaders who could lead the city through the difficult and wonderful years ahead. We knew this was a challenge but we also knew that true leaders thrive on challenge.

The School of the New Millennium has been in existence for seven years, with 500 students in grades K–12. From the beginning we have been recognized as the unique institution we are. We have been featured in *Best Public Middle Schools in New York* and students from all over the city apply to us.

Our school will submit a proposal to the Chancellor later this year to become one of the first public charter schools in the city. Our school is a little family with heavy involvement on the part of the parents. When the charter goes through, the parents—the people who really know what's best for their kids—will have even more involvement in the running of the school. . . .

## OUR PHILOSOPHY . . .

**Students** develop into leaders when they feel safe and known and when they are challenged to do their best. Big institutions can be alienating and the special qualities of each child can be lost. Instead we try to run our school like a family. In a family, every member gets understanding and support and when someone has a problem, we all work together to solve it. So it is at New Millennium . . . At New Millennium, teachers team-teach, classes are arranged in clusters, parents volunteer, and decisions are made after thorough dialogue with many people. . . .

## WHAT WE STUDY . . .

**We** study New York City. Traditional subjects are related as much as possible to the study of the land, history, technology, economics, culture, and people of New York. Since the arts are so central to New York, all students have a daily arts class. . . . When our students become the leaders of tomorrow, they will be prepared. They will know the city of today and yesterday and thus be ready to form the city of the future.

Students work on both individual and group projects that introduce them to the work world of the 21st century. Classes take frequent field trips, exploring all the city has to offer.

Students also participate in learning about their school and their community by service within the school and community. Older students work in local companies and volunteer in community groups to gain life experience. . . .

Our family of the School of the New Millennium is looking toward the future with confidence.

—from an informational pamphlet on
the School of the New Millennium

Monday morning, I find myself on the number-seven train to Queens.

Seven is a lucky number, and the number-seven train is a mighty good train. It burrows beneath the avenues of Manhattan, through the chic black of tunnel, the always-in-fashion simplicity of stone, under the river, before it comes up again. It's a roller coaster, the seven. The first curve on the trestle and the passengers—the lady in the sari, the kid with the Walkman, the man sleepily munching a seeded roll—half fall out of their seats. And then we're off. Rattling by those homely stops no one has ever written songs about—*I'll take Vernon Jackson, and Queens Plaza, too*—while I look out at the houses facing the railroad tracks, the Irish pubs, the signs in Spanish and Hindi, the billboard for a dental clinic featuring smiling people with too many teeth and weird necks, and behind them, in the distance, the imperial knives of Manhattan gleaming.

I am going home.

I don't care what the man says. You *can* go home again. It's like one of those electronic bracelets released prisoners wear. You haul water out of a mountain stream, you find yourself in Barcelona or Judith Gap, you have learned the Montenegrin words for *To Your Health,* and *Jump,* and used them, too; you have congratulated yourself on the brilliance of your escape, but the bracelet is always there, ready to let you know you have strayed too far, and one day it does: *Beep. Beep. Beep.* How else can I explain it? I am sitting on the number-seven train, barreling through Queens, staring at a little girl who looks so much like I once did— short, plump, rosy-cheeked, straggling long brown hair—that I almost pull the emergency cord, shout that I've been kidnapped, and *She, she—that one picking at her scab—she did it.*

I am going to a neighborhood not far from my old neighborhood. The humble slope of those streets, streets of my childhood, are still embedded in me. How odd. How mysterious. And wait, the Great Return gets weirder still: for those dreams I sometimes have, when I discover that I neglected to take that math test in the ninth grade, that all my education has been declared null and void, that I must take my old seat again and sit through another lifetime of margins and isosceles triangles? Those dreams, it turns out, have come to pass.

I am going back to school.

Even more bizarre: I'm looking forward to it.

Kind of, I guess. Sort of. Well, to be honest . . .

Maybe.


Saturday morning, the one before last, I was sitting in my kitchen, lolling about in my old nightgown, when the phone rang.

I was scared of the phone ringing.

I had been semi-employed for months, long enough to have bills I was having trouble paying. And when you have trouble paying your bills, you get depressed, and then you pick up your phone and call buddies in D.C. and California and talk about how depressed you are, and yes, I know, such behavior is in no way sensible, adding as it does to the enormity of the bills, and probably I require years of expensive therapy to cure it, but there you are: I was scared of the phone ringing, but also wanted it to ring, hoping it would be some sympathetic soul ready to lovingly discuss my depression.

"Yes?" said I.

"May I speak to Elizabeth Gold?"

This was bad, this was very bad. This was a male stranger asking for me. That could only mean one thing. He was going to demand his money.

"She's not here," I said. And then, chirpily, roommate style: "Want to leave a message?"

"Yes. Tell her this is Leon Greene at the School of the New Millennium."

*Now I've done it.*

I am a fool. It had never occurred to me that if I sent résumés *out*, an answer might come *in*. I had just been sticking them in envelopes merely as little acts of faith, little candles lit. I hadn't really imagined that someone would actually read the damn things. And like it. But here was the evidence. I had found this book called something like *The Best Public Middle Schools in New York*. I had written to almost all of them. And now, Leon Greene, at the School of the New Millennium, wanted to speak to me.

And what had I done? Told him in my very own voice that She Was Not Here.

I took a deep breath. "Let me get a pencil," I said. But halfway through scribbling the message I suddenly exhaled.

"Actually," I said, "I *am* Elizabeth Gold."

*Now I've really really done it.*

Or so I thought.

"Oh, that's good," he said. "We wanted to talk to you. We read your résumé, and we liked it a lot. Could you come in today?"

I could. I did. And as for why he didn't ask me why I would pretend to be not here, the answer is simple: He didn't want to know.

Of course not. Why would he want to know? We were sitting there, in the office of the School of the New Millennium, Leon and the Parents Committee and me, all of us smiling. That foolish little blind-date smile you wear when you discover, Thank God, that the One across the table, improbable as it seems, actually has something in common with you: a taste for Cabernet, perhaps, or water skiing. In this case, what we shared was simple. They needed to hire someone. I needed to be hired.

If only all relationships were so easy.

Leon Greene looked like Mr. Toad from *The Wind in the Willows*.

He looked remarkably like Mr. Toad, short, a little goggle-eyed, with the rounded, waistless physique so common among principals, as if, the way the Japanese must take their shoes off before entering the house, they have to unlace their bones and muscle before coming in the door. That is the price to pay for Authority. Not that it mattered. I didn't want to go out with this man. I wanted to be paid by him. While a little bit of sexual harassment, by the right person anyway, in my current state of mind, would probably have been a very nice thing, it was not my first requirement. So he talked, and I beamed, and as he kept talking, I beamed more and more, as if I were discovering that it was not just Cabernet, thank you very much, but '94, from a vineyard only few had heard of, and water skiing done backwards, with triple axles and quadruple flips.

"So," Leon Greene said. "What do you want to know about the School of the New Millennium?"

"Everything," I said.

He commenced.

He told me things, some of which I already knew. But I let him tell me again, while I nodded and smiled at all the right moments. He told me how some children in the New York City system were getting a very good education, and some a very bad; how classes were too large, bureaucracy too great, how children needed to feel loved, and safe, in order to learn anything. He told me how some teachers and parents had gotten together, less than ten years before, and formed a school that would provide all this, and utilize all the wonderful resources of the metropolis around it. He told me that the school was a *family*, which is why it went from kindergarten all the way to twelfth. That way there were big brothers and sisters and little brothers and sisters. We, the teachers, were part of the family, too. That is why we were all on a first-name basis here. None of that old-fashioned Mr. and Miss; equals all, that's who we were. He told me that our mission was to develop New York's future leaders. He told me our students' self-esteem was crucial. He told me every child had a voice. He told me we must love all the children, equally.

"Can you do that?" he asked.

"Sure I can," I answered.

"This is a class that needs a lot of love," he said. "They've had nothing but bad luck. They started out with Sharon. A wonderful teacher, a science teacher who decided to switch to English. Then she got sick. Then we got April. She's a dance teacher, but she has a B.A. in English, so that's all right. Then *she* got sick. Then we had Natalie sub for us for a few weeks, but what a relief: here you are. A permanent teacher. They'll be so happy to see you."

"Great," I said.

"I have just one question," he added, and my heart sank a little. This was the moment in the blind date when it was no longer Cabernet and water skiing. This was the moment when he would lean across the table, and take my hand, and whisper softly: *How do you feel about men in pink garter belts?* Or, *Do you love Goebbels the way I do?*

"How are you with discipline?" he said.

Discipline. I had spent my whole career avoiding it. What does someone who writes poetry and lives in an illegal sublet in a midtown tenement know about discipline—either keeping it or having it? It was a miracle, as far as I was concerned, that I didn't weigh five hundred pounds and that I brushed my teeth every day.

"Oh, I'm great with it," I said.

"Discipline is important," he said. "It's not about yelling, and it's not about size, either. It's certainly not about fear. It's about . . . *authority.* Yes, authority. It's something poor April had. She's just in her early twenties, and weighs only about a hundred pounds, but when she spoke, her students listened. And they loved her. They really did. No matter.

"I'm sure they'll love you, too."

. . .

So that is how I come to be sitting here, Monday morning on the number seven train, a slim folder of slim poems in my lap. Congratulations, I think, are in order: I have done it. I have gone down to the Board of Ed in downtown Brooklyn, I have handed in forms 2B and 12C, I have kept my pink paper separate from the yellow, and I am now on my way to being a responsible person. A person who sends kids on *their* ways to being responsible people. I have emerged from the gloom of 110 Livingston Street, that dark museum of nineteenth-century bureaucracy, where papers are stamped and stamped again and then, I suspect, forgotten. And now, trying to quiet those first-day nerves, I tell myself what everyone seems to be telling me: *They will love you.*

In a day or two, April, that delicate authoritarian, will be forgotten, and *I* will be that cool teacher opening up their brains and hearts to the greater world. Even Pancho, the boy scowling in the back, the one with the knife scar on his cheek, will one day come round. He'll brush his lank hair out of his eyes and confess his sorrows, and the next thing you know, we've got him on a full scholarship to Harvard, while he mumbles, *It's all because of her. She believed in me.*

*They will love me.* And of course it seems ridiculous, to hope that an anonymous group of kids will love me, but try being in a room full of people who feel the opposite. People who are younger, and probably stronger, and bigger than you.

And now it is my stop. I leap up, and run down the stairs past the lady yelling *baterías, baterías, baterías,* and the other crying *tamales, tamales, tamales,* I walk past the Fruitytopia, and La Casa Del Zapatos de Buster Brown, and the restaurant where a few years ago a crusading Colombian journalist got himself shot down. When I was growing up, this was a neighborhood of Jewish dentists. And now? Here we are. New Millennium. Somehow the places and things I thought I knew have transformed themselves, when I wasn't paying attention, mango by mango, into the Future. Another place altogether, where I am supposed to lead.

It is a nice day, warm and springlike, and along the homely streets of low brick apartment houses, the forsythia is doing its confused precocious forsythia thing: blooming. In February. And now I am at the school. A bland white box, a former department store.

Outside the teenagers are gathering. City kids. Kids of every color. Boys in baggy jeans. Girls in skin-tight Lycra pants. Gossiping, cigarette smoking, Walkman playing, skateboard balancing, youth machines.

I feel old. This is not a pleasant feeling. And little. Shriveled, let's say, since we're feeling so old. Five feet two inches of antiquated muscle and bone, and *okay*, flab.

The girls are talking. *She did that to me and I did that to her and then she had the NERVE to do that to me and what do you think I did? I had NO CHOICE but to do that to her and*

*It's not fair,* the boys are saying, *It's not fair, it's not fair*

*They will love me,* I tell myself. *How could they not love me? Am I not just like them? Really, truly, like them? I also think it's Not Fair. Hell, I know it's not. Whatever it is, It's Not Fair. It can't be.*

But it doesn't matter, because even as I'm giving myself this pep talk, last night's conversation is running through my head.

I had called Leon, as he had instructed, to discuss this Monday morning.

"So," he said. "What are you going to do the first day?"

"I have some poems," I said. "We'll read them, we'll talk about them, and then we'll write our own."

A silence. "Remember," he said, "plan carefully. Whatever you do, you win them, or lose them, for the rest of the year, in the first five minutes."

"Oh."

"But just relax."

"Oh." Then I took a breath, and asked the question I needed to ask. "Look, what exactly is my status here? Is April coming back?"

"No. She's not coming back. She's quite ill. You're their teacher now."

"Okay."

"The first five minutes. Remember that."

march
**family (see dysfunctional)**

ONE HUNDRED YEARS FROM NOW

IT WILL NOT MATTER

WHAT KIND OF CAR I DROVE,

WHAT KIND OF HOUSE I LIVED IN,

HOW MUCH MONEY I HAD

IN MY BANK ACCOUNT,

NOR WHAT MY CLOTHES LOOKED LIKE.

BUT THE WORLD MAY BE

A LITTLE BETTER

BECAUSE I WAS IMPORTANT

IN THE LIFE OF A CHILD.

—Sign in the School of the New Millennium office

*day one. or day twelve. tuesday. or wednesday. 9:15. or 2:00. or what is this thing called day, and what is an hour, and what is a minute, when i have entered this place where time has no meaning, stuck in the eternal present, yes it has happened, i took the number- seven train, one little swipe of the metro card, and i walked past the tamale lady, and maybe this was my mistake, maybe i should have bought something from the tamale lady, maybe this was the test i failed, the way maidens in fairy stories don't give a cup of cool water to the crone they met and end up spitting up frogs for the rest of their lives, i must be paying for something, what other explanation could there be?*

This is Hell. I never believed in it before, but now the evidence is in. The screaming. The hitting. The grunting. ("Is that you or your students?" a friend of mine quips, when I tell her this, and except for the hitting, I'd have to answer, we at the School of the New Millennium are a little family, we like to do things together.)

And the hooting, don't forget the hooting, there is a boy over there who likes to hoot like a screech owl—when he's not, that is, beating his head for his own amusement against the metal file cabinets. And the screaming. Did I mention the screaming? The noise that never stops? And the heat, and the stink? And the look in their eyes of souls in torment, because after all, they are still children, and some of them want it to be different, and don't know how to make it different, and I can do nothing for them? Nothing, nothing. Nothing.

I am not really thinking. In the midst of this roar, that is not what I'm capable of doing; all I'm doing is obeying this voice, Her Master's Voice, which says, *Sit Here. Sit Here. Don't Move. Don't Flee. Sit. Sit,* and my obedience is a triumph of the will. Still, something buried deep inside my body, some remnant of amphibian brain, is doing something *resembling* thinking, is saying, *My Fault, My Fault, I did this, I did this, with every little misstep, every little swerve to the left instead of the right, I was coming closer and closer, to this,* and I blink in the cold white light of the room and the stink, that rank *Eau de Tomcat,* is getting stronger, and I realize, ashamed, that the smell is coming from *me*. It is the smell of terror, the smell of the soul trapped in the body and the body trapped in a room, it is the animal smell of No Escape, it is my confession. No one needs to ask how I'm doing. They just need to smell me, and they'll know.

How did things get so bad? I don't know, and I'll never know. Was it something buried in me in the womb, or before that, some ancestral blur in judgment, some terrible Polish mistake? Or was it later than that? Did it begin in the Board of Ed, or on my first morning, when I stood there, shyly, in the office, as the teachers did their xeroxing, and one of them, trying to be friendly, said, "Oh, poor thing, so *you're* the new ninth-grade teacher, good luck, they've been killing off teachers since the eighth"? Was it then? Or when Tom, twenty-five years old, and supremely confident, the American history teacher, and also the dean, walked me up the stairs to Room 313 and made the speech that worked wonders: "This is Elizabeth, and she is your real teacher," he said.

"Understand? I know some of you are going to want to treat her like a sub. But believe me, she's not. She is going to teach a real class and give you real homework and give you real grades, and if you act up, there will be real consequences. Any questions?"

No questions. Some of them knew, without saying a word, exactly what was going to commence.

I look out, that first day, at all the evidence I need of Nature's nasty comic spirit: the well-developed girls, womanly girls ( I read somewhere that girls are developing earlier and earlier, and from this vantage point, it seems that way). Girls who radiate, and maybe it is false bravado, remarkable physical assurance. And the boys. There's not one you would call *manly*. Skinny boys. Boys lost in swagger-fashionable boy clothes of the moment: baggy jeans, loose T-shirts. Ghetto clothes, or imitation ghetto clothes. Boys with acne. Boys with their first dark down staining their lips. Or not even that. My charges. Women, in body, anyway, and boys.

*God*, I think. *I have no idea what I'm doing.*

But I think it authoritatively, in the calm center of my being, I think that, and I open my mouth, and I might as well be opening it not to speak but to show off my dental fillings, because it begins.

It begins in 9B, the first class of my day, my homeroom class. It begins when Ricardo Silva, in the back of the room, waits for Tom to go and then whips out a can of soda and smirks at me. He's not supposed to drink soda in the classroom. *No food, no drinks, no Walkman, no hats, no do-rags*, I was told this very carefully, this was part of my job of keeping order, and though personally I could care less if he drinks soda or not, I have taken this job, and so it is important.

Be a general, Leon has told me, and so in the spirit of Lee or Washington or maybe Douglas MacArthur I very kindly, yet firmly, ask Ricardo to stop drinking that soda.

He takes a nice refreshing gulp, *and this is boring,* I think to myself. Here he is, being a teenager, challenging me. Couldn't he be less predictable and quote Latin instead?

And now Ricardo Silva and I are having the last discussion in the world I want to be having—about why he won't put away that soda—and both of us are getting more heated, and everyone in the class is taking bets—will he or won't he stop drinking that soda?—and the sound is bubbling up, it is time for me to take control. I grab the can out of his hand.

"Give me my soda!"

"At the end of class."

"Give me my soda!"

"At the end of class."

"Give me my soda!"

"No."

"Give me my soda!"

"No."

"Soda! Soda! SoDA! GIVE. ME. MY. SODA."

*"No."*

"Give this MAN his soda!"

"No."

"You owe me money. You took my soda. Give me my soda. Give this MAN his soda!"

"No."

"Give this MAN his soda!"

"No."

"GIVE THIS MAN HIS SODA!"

"I will give this *boy* his soda at the end of class."

*Ooooh,* says the class.

And now, of course, this boy has transformed me into the kind of adult I can't stand. The kind of adult who cares about soda. Not that there isn't this little voice inside me whispering, Oh come on, let him have his soda. Drink up, Ricardo, drink up. Work on those cavities. Flaunt that manhood.

But give in to that voice, and I'm lost.

Our struggle is not about soda, anyway. It's about the semiotics of soda. That's what it is, and I know that's what it is. It's not the soda, but what the soda *means.* That's why he's drinking it. That's why I'm supposed to take it away. And yet. I just can't care, but school is a place of symbols, the way all institutions are, and already I'm losing that battle. So swept up in the semiotics of soda and chewing gum and hats I can hardly think.

While this is going on, I am trying to figure out what exactly it is the students have been learning, and reading, because despite my friendly interview, this is something no one in the administration seems to know. What does the school expect me to do here? More, surely, than discussing soda. I start to give my class a writing assignment; an exercise that leads into the next exercise, but when people are yelling and punching and challenging my authority, we never seem to get where I thought we would go. And I'm telling myself, this too will pass, they're getting used to me, they're acting out, and no bell rings, for we in the School of the New Millennium don't believe in bells, but Time to Go is Time to Go and in one Pavlovian moment they rise to their feet and head out the door, and I, *remarkable,* in the silence after they go, am trembling.

Simply from going through what is, after all, the ordinary lot for many a human being: standing in a class, and trying to teach someone something, and not completely knowing what you are doing. This is not Everest we're talking about. This is ordinary, and I, little *wuss,* am trembling.

Then 9A rolls into the room. The best class, in terms of ability, anyway, for though we're not officially tracked at the School of the New Millennium, the truth is, 9A is where most of the students who manage to pass end up. It is someone in 9A who tells me this, though sooner or later I would have figured it out. Just because it is agreed that we are all equals here and that the weak ones are helped by the strong, doesn't mean that the parents of the students in 9A want their children to be hanging around with Ricardo Silva, a seventeen-year-old who barely knows what a fraction is.

And, of course, drinks a lot of soda.

Eighty-four minutes.

The latest research has shown that a longer class period gives students and teachers more time for intellectual exploration, and so a longer class period—eighty-four minutes as opposed to the standard fifty—it is.

The roar begins. For it is true that 9A is my best class. That just makes them more competitive. In everything.

As a girl in the back turns up her Walkman so loud I can hear it across the room, I meet the eyes of Eric Antonelli, a small, slight boy with an elfin, serious, almost transparent face. "Was it always like this?" I say.

"Actually," says Eric, "with April it was a little worse."

Ken, a Japanese boy who spends most of his time with his

head resting on his arm, in a state, seemingly, of deep philosophical contemplation, suddenly looks up. "Why don't you call the office? That's what Sharon did."

Ah, Sharon. The first one to sicken and leave. What I can't understand about this part of the story is that there is a system-wide shortage of science teachers, but somehow she got shoehorned into teaching English, because it was assumed, I guess, that anyone breathing could do it.

Sharon showed them movies about Hiroshima and had them write about it. *Nuclear radiation is bad. In this paper, I will prove why it is bad.*

The students loved her. They loved her a lot, Leon has told me.

"Yes," says Ken. "Call the office. Sharon did that. Every day, if she had to."

"Every day?" I ask. "Did it work?"

"For a little while," says Ken.

At least it makes a change to call the office, so I do. No one answers, and as I hang up, Eric offers a piece of advice.

"Just teach the ones who want to listen, and ignore the rest. That's what everybody else does."

Everybody else is a trooper, then. For I cannot; I cannot think in this din, and if I can't think, I can't teach.

No matter. When I sneak a look at my watch, I see rescue is coming: it's time for lunch.

Thank God for our frail human bodies, the whorls and complaints of our digestive systems. The class gets up to go and I drift out with it, and stumble down to the ground floor.

At the main entrance, Nkruma, our handsome and dashing global history teacher, and the unofficial king of the school, is standing among a cluster of students, practicing the major form of discipline we've got: lunch.

Yes, if a student is bad, if he chews gum, plays Walkman, does no homework, shaves head in class, tattoos limbs of student in the next seat, a teacher can hand in a list and this student will be forbidden to go out to lunch. It's school cafeteria food for you, Charlie, it's the basement, where nutritive mounds of Something are eaten beneath the student mural (do we see a pattern beginning to emerge?) dedicated to the First Dead Teacher of the School of the New Millennium.

"Cindy? Can't go out there, I'm afraid."

"But my health! I'm on a restricted diet!"

"No. David, you can go."

"Nkruma. *Please.*"

"No, Cindy. No. Nothing to discuss. Orlando . . . you can go. Nestor . . . I'm sorry."

"*Nkruma.*"

"Ken, you can go. Natasha, you can go. Tiffany . . . sorry."

"Please. Please. Please."

"I'm going to get her! I'm going to *get* her!"

"Nestor? You want to say that again?"

"*Man . . .*"

"Sarah, yes. Silvia yes, Ahmed, yes . . ."

I push past them all, and Nkruma gives me a little smile. "How's it going?"

*Sugar,* I think.

My mouth is filled with a sour juice that tastes as if scraped up from a hidden crevice in my gut, and it probably has been. This is probably the taste of a baby ulcer. No time to see a doctor. But somewhere in Jackson Heights, sugar is out there.

In my days as a teenage compulsive reader, plowing through great volumes, the more ponderous and self-serious the better, I came upon, on the library shelves, *Buddenbrooks*, a dreadful book, really, but there is one scene I remember. One of the members of this terrible family is a diabetic who commits suicide by eating a dozen jelly doughnuts. They find him lying on the floor of his apartment, an empty box beside him, a ring of powdered sugar around his lips. What a glorious way to go. Class 9C is just around the corner. A dozen jelly doughnuts please, and step on it.

When I first entered the public school system as an adult, I used to wonder why there were always so many tubby adults waddling around. Now I know.

Sugar, I think; oil, great rivulets of it. I hie myself to the coffee shop across the street.

It is the teacher hangout, and also the hangout for one quiet, serious junior, drinking her coffee with ladylike sips while day-dreaming over the Harvard catalogue. No one else goes there, it is so hopelessly square, so old-fashioned American Coffee Shop, circa 1970 or so. It smells like my childhood, vinyl, and yes, sugar, and to sit there is to feel relieved of adult weight.

My pants are getting tight.

I am accumulating adult weight.

No matter. I gobble apple crumb cake or spoon hot pea soup into my mouth. I've got fortifying to do.

9C lies ahead, the class of extravagant failures, of those who have been classified, because we don't know how else to classify them, as learning disabled. Also the class of quiet immigrant children whose parents are too civilized and too cowed to complain.

9C. There's glitter to its chaos, a Liberace in Las Vegas chaos. Compared to 9C, every other class is simply banging out "Heart and Soul" on the sleep-away camp piano. 9C has no patience with amateurs. It knows how to dish out the real thing.

But perhaps a little demonstration is in order:

"HOMO."

"HOMO. HOMO. HOMO."

Is this a confession? A suggestion? A celebration of our diversity? All The Different and Wonderful Ways We Are?

"HOMO. HOMO. HOMO."

*Damn.* It's good to be back. Every student, after all, has a voice. How swell that this one is using it.

"*HOMO. HOMO.*"

Sometimes I just sit back and watch. And listen. When I'm not yelling, I sit back and take it in. It's so much better that way. If someone is going to say *Fuck you,* better it is said to someone else, because I'm tired of *fuck you.* I've had a lifetime of *fuck you,* but these youths are just beginning to fill up on it, so why, in this capitalist society, should I stop them? They've got satiation to reach.

"*Fuck you.*"

"*NO. Fuck you. Fuck* you!"

"*Fuck you. Fuck you.*"

A jelly doughnut would be just the thing right now.

"HOMO. HOMO."

Though there's something worse than noise: Silence.

The silence of Sammy Morales, it's dangerous silence. It's the silence when you close your eyes and say, *I don't want to watch.*

But I have to, for I am in the presence of mystery.

The mystery of sex, that bubble in the blood. I too have felt it, I think I remember that. How strange, how inexplicable, that one mouth opening, *this* mouth, instead of *that* mouth—too bad this is not biology class. Then we could discuss why someone like Sammy Morales is so irresistible to certain girls, and I must say, certain girls, but still. *What does he have? What does he have?* A little groping's going on, a canoodling of the hair, are they going to kiss? *Please, please, I pray, don't let them kiss, I don't want to tell them to unglue those lips, and Tongues, Buster, Are Not For Sharing,* but the other part of me is thinking, *Why not kiss?* Who am I to interfere with young love, if that's what it is? Why don't I push a couple of desks together in the back and throw a sheet over them, light some mood candles (though they don't really *need* mood candles), toss over a pack of cigarettes for after, why don't I make myself useful?

Tiffany is painting her long blue nails, laughing her manic laugh, banging her forehead on the desk with the force of it, and a couple of girls are bopping away to whatever's playing on their Walkmans, and a wrestling magazine is eagerly passed from hand to hand. "I hate Elizabeth!" Samantha shouts, and self-expression is a great thing, Luisa thinks so, too. "I hate her, too," she says, and *Walkmans off, hats off, do-rags off,* oh, I'm making the attempt, the feeble attempt, *Pizza away, magazine away, candy away, tranquilizers away* (actually, if there were any tranquilizers, they would have to be handed to me, immediately), and Jennifer's hitting Anthony and Anthony, Luis, it's all in fun, kids, and here is Jose, in an act of pure spiritual detachment, lying across the desks with a sweater over his head.

While this is going on, some students have turned on the computers that Leon is so proud of and are working on the technological skills that will zip them straight to the World of Tomorrow.

They're playing solitaire.

Solitaire. How delicious, a game for one. Oh, for a good game of solitaire, sitting in a train perhaps, a train speeding through some empty blue silent place, a Scottish moor at twilight, a nice glass of Glenfiddich at my side, *No, make it a bottle, sounds good to me, kids, can I join you?* and then Randolph notices that I have stopped paying him the attention he deserves, so, time to opine again:

"HOMO. *HOMO.*"

What a remarkable voice that boy has. Is he channeling Caruso, that his voice should be so ringing and so powerful?

"HOMO."

He confuses me, Randolph does. The very first day I walked in, I was struck by the princely bones in his face, his dark mahogany skin, and his eyes, secret wells of smarts and kindness. You can read a face, you really can, and even while Randolph shouts and hits and flings himself about, his eyes seem to be looking out and quietly conversing: *This is not really me,* those eyes seem to be saying, *this is somebody else, and will somebody please stop him.*

"HOMO. HOMO. HOMO. HOMO. HO MO."

Sammy Morales stops what he is doing and cackles with laughter.

"HOMO. HOMO. HOMO."

I call the office. No one answers. Maybe I'm the one who should put a sweater on my head.

"JOSE IS A HOMO!"

Oh Christ.

Luckily Jose doesn't speak much English. He actually shouldn't even be here at all. He should be doing full-time ESL. This is a blessing.

It is my fault. It is all my fault. Who else's could it be?

You see, I need to love them. That is what Leon would say. I need to love *all* of them with a pure unconditional love that God might envy, and if only I could, *really* could, it would radiate from my brow and Randolph would stop shouting *Homo* and join Act Up instead.

*HOMO,* and in the spirit of collaboration, Sammy Morales joins him. Isn't it great, kids, when we work together? The din is formidable: *JOSE IS A HOMO.*

Now the class is rising. Not, thank God, to work on their choral piece, to riff on all the syllabic possibilities of *Jose* and *Homo,* but to go.

Only one period left, and that one has no students in it. It's my preparation period, or to be honest, recovery period. No matter what they call it, it's time for 9C to leave. And as the students file out, and I sit there, shaking, Miriam shows up.

She is the economics teacher, a tall, slim, elegant black woman with a cropped haircut and an air of natural repose. Almost nothing seems to ruffle her.

For the next eighty-four minutes, this will be her classroom.

"How's it going?" she says.

# HOW CAN I GET MY CLASS BACK?

1. Monday: fill out cards with numbers
2. call parents
3. new seating chart
4. not on time, no supplies, don't do their work, talk back, call out, wear hat, throw something, eat, chew gum, sleep, do nothing—call parents
5. What is expected of them every day:

   Journal
   Instruction: Grammar, writing—I need to make charts
   Handwriting—1 letter a day
   Autobiography project: I need a proposal of what they are going to do in terms of poetry, illustration, collage, song lyrics, flashbacks

   Monday: Prewriting and 1st draft—conference with a friend with your first draft—turn in (I just check it) VOCABULARY

   Tuesday: give back 2nd draft—revise ideas, content—don't worry about grammar yet. They hold on to it—can put it in their folder. GRAMMAR

   Wednesday: descriptive writing, excerpts from movies, excerpts from books, group discussions about pieces of autobiographies

   Thursday: I hand back their 2nd draft. This time they have to edit for punctuation, grammar, and spelling. They conference with a friend. The work gets done with different pens. They turn it in. GRAMMAR

   Friday: I give them back their 2nd draft with rewrites. On Friday the class writes their final 3rd draft. VOCABULARY TEST END OF CLASS—end with class lottery—anyone whose parent I haven't called, haven't pulled their lunch card, can put their name into the class lottery for a CD. Also end the week with . . .

—note discovered in April's lesson plan book

I have done it.

It is my first Friday, and I am still standing. As 9B troops out the door, and I lean over my desk, breathing deep, Peter Garcia comes up to me.

"Hi," he says. He gives me his hand to shake, and a sheet of paper. "Here's the homework you asked for."

I look it over. He has a clear, concise style without many mistakes; the style of a boy who knows where he's going and would like to get there as soon as possible. "Not bad," I say.

"Oh, I'm lazy," he says. "I'm very lazy."

I'm looking at Peter Garcia; his round, pale face, his cloud of curly dark hair, his round dark eyes, his clothes so extravagantly teenage baggy there is no way I can tell if he is plump or thin, and I think, maybe it's true. That paper has the mark of a smart boy writing with one hand tied behind his back.

"I've just figured how to do enough to get by," he says.

The temptation to say, *Well, honey, so do we all, sometimes,* is very strong, but it is early in the year, so instead I find myself simply smiling and smiling at Peter Garcia, saying nothing at all.


It is time for lunch. It is Thursday, or Friday, the first week, or the second, and as the students of 9A rise as one organism to leave, one remains. It is Adam Patel, the boy who sits in the back of the room. He walks up to my desk and says hello.

Adam is childishly slight, and his baggy jeans make him seem even slimmer, lost in a big man's clothes. His skin is dark, that Indian dark that is almost black. His features are fine and regular. He wears round gold-rimmed John Lennon glasses, and his black hair, parted in the middle, and unfashionably long, falls in loose waves about his thin face.

This is a boy for the barricades, but there is no barricade in sight.

"A little chaotic in here," I say, just to let him know I'm no fool. I've noticed.

"Of course it is," says Adam Patel. "They can't help it. They've been corrupted by the system."

"Really?" I say.

"Yes." He tucks a tress behind one ear, something he does when excited or concentrating hard. "The system doesn't want kids to think. That's too dangerous. We might start asking too many questions. Like what it is we're learning and why we're learning it?"

"I'm with you," I say. "But how can you understand even the simplest thing when it's never quiet? You can't talk about anything interesting or smart in a room full of screaming people."

"We've just got to start all over," he says. "That's what we've got to do."

"Okay."

"Listen. I've been reading these guys—have you heard of them? Herbert Kohl, Jonathan Kozol, and they say—"

But I'm not quite listening. I've read them, or enough of them, to know what they say. I'm thinking instead about Adam Patel, this boy in the back who has discovered a way of keeping his mind alive. It occurs to me that he is exactly the kind of boy I would have had a major crush on in high school. But he would have been too cool, too self-assured, for someone like me. That's what I would have thought.

All during lunch period, Adam tells me about the education system. He tells me how it destroys your individuality, your integrity, your heart. He tells me how it is just in the business of developing mindless consumers, and if students act up, it is just a form of rebellion. I begin to tell him he is not the first person to think this, but then I change my mind. It is too much of a relief to simply listen.

He pauses for breath, and then starts up again.

"Listen," he says, "when I get older, I'm going to reform the education system. I know how to do it. Maybe, when I tell you, you'll think it's crazy, but I *know* this idea can work. It's a radical idea. A great idea! And it's *never* been tried before."

"Really?" I say. "What is it?"

"We're going to have free, and interesting, and creative discussions," says Adam Patel.


Sarah Patel, in 9C, sits where most of the first- or second-generation immigrant children sit, in the front row, as far from the punching and noise as possible. She is no relation to Adam, though they are both dark, both thin.

How pretty she is, Sarah Patel. It is the first thing I notice. It is impossible not to. Many of my girl students, of course, are pretty, but Sarah is different. While a lot of her peers swagger around the school in the tiniest tops and the tightest pants, oozing sexual confidence (real or an act, I cannot say), Sarah is simply, like a girl in a fairy tale, pretty. Her thick black hair tumbles down her back, her eyes are huge and luminous, and her smile is spontaneous and without guile. If she knew the power of that beauty, she could be a dangerous girl, but if she knew that power, she would not be Sarah Patel.

"Oh," she says, the first day, when I come in, "a new English teacher. Another one. I hope you're going to be nice. The last teacher was *so nice.*"

"I hope I'm going to be nice, too."

"I hope it's not going to be boring. English this year, it's just been boring. Filling in workbooks. Watching movies about Hiroshima. That's not English! I love English. It's my favorite subject."

Who would not beam at this young girl, not only so beautiful, but so intelligent, and with such good taste?

Sarah Patel befriends me. I have no idea why. She sees me come into class, she sees me open my mouth and hears the roar start up, she sees me fail and fail and fail and still, she befriends me. One day she comes up to me and confides in me a bit, and I listen, and next thing you know, Sarah Patel and I are hanging out in the hall, before class begins, having girl-to-girl discussions about life.

Could it possibly be that Sarah Patel is so confused she thinks of me as her role model?

Whatever her reasons, I'm enjoying this. I always wanted a kid sister, and in this most unlikely of places, I seem to have acquired a surrogate one.

And now she is staring at me. Impossible not to revert to my old adolescent insecurity under the gaze of this beautiful young girl, but she is not thinking what I am thinking.

"Are you wearing colored contacts?" she says.

"No."

"You mean those are your *real* eyes?"

"Sure are."

"They're all different colors."

"Yeah, I know. And they change color, depending on what I'm wearing. Or what the weather is like. They'll look gray, or blue, or green."

"Wow," she says, "they're *pretty.*"

"Well, thank you," I say, while part of me thinks this is not a typical teacher-student discussion, and glad I am for it, and another part of me is thinking, that despite myself I am pleased that she noticed, and It's an odd lot, being a girl, Sarah Patel. To care so much, to hope someone notices our eyes are pretty.

Sarah has another question.

"Elizabeth," she says, "what would you rather have, a brilliant career or true love?"

I sigh. How could such a guileless girl ask such discomforting questions? How to choose, when I have neither, and desperately crave both?

"Oh, *I* don't know," I say.

"I'll take the brilliant career," she says. "That's what lasts. As for you—it's true love, isn't it, Elizabeth?"

"True love would be an okay thing," I say. "It would be *more* than okay. But the brilliant career would be, too."

And she's about to open her mouth and ask me another question. Some other terrifying question that will start me wondering what in hell went wrong. Not that that is her intention. She sees me as an adult; ergo, I know what I'm doing.

"HOMO. HOMO. HOMO."

"Lay off me, you fucking lesbian."

"Oh fuck. I hate this class."

I look at my watch. "Time to start," I say.


"I *love* you!"

Amy Lee, a Chinese student in 9C, flings her arms about my waist and gives me a big hug.

I find this a little weird.

"You are a *good* teacher. You are the best teacher."

It is the first week, or maybe the second, and in the back David and Alan are staging a firefight with plastic monsters complete with sound effects, and Sammy Morales is doing his Barry White imitation, and Randolph is yodeling a *HOMO* or two, just to keep the uvula in shape, and Amy, a little slip of a thing, so small and delicate she makes me feel positively gallumphing, is standing in the middle of this, admiring my teaching ability.

"Thank you," I say. What else can I say?

"The best, the best," she says, while I am trying, gently, gently, don't want to damage her self-esteem, to unpeel her.

What is going on in that girl's mind I cannot imagine. This is not the kind of thing I did in ninth grade. I was low on flinging. I would no more have thought of embracing Miss Mealy than asking her to waltz. As for Mr. Malinowski. Miss Safka, Miss Maish, Mrs. . . . I know this sounds improbable . . . Love.

God. How she disliked me.

Maybe I erred in stinting on my praise, but hands off was easy.

"*Oh*. I love you so so much."

"Hey. Love you, too," I say.

Leon would say that our school is a family, but I find that confusing. Who's the uncle here? The mad aunt, the second cousin once removed? The kink in the family tree no one talks about? No. This is no family. Families get to take trips in the car, while Father, in his pleasant off-key baritone, sings "Summertime" and the kids ask over and over again if we're there yet. Families go to Jones Beach and the mountains, they go out for Chinese, they go to Fourth of July picnics where the older kids instruct the younger ones about how babies are made. Families get around, they meet other families, they have meaningful discussions, they tell good and bad jokes. There are other things, too, some of them, of course, not so jolly, but still. If this is a family, this is not my family. It's that family down the block whose yard is littered with broken washing machines. It's the family with the son who prowls the neighborhood at night, strangling cats.

I prefer to think of this place not as a family but a country, an isolated mountain nation. A place that feels far away from anything I would call ordinary life, but of course I am wrong. The borders of this place are porous. Its citizens leave every evening, and make their way back in, heavily weighted with everything they bring from home.

I'm paying a different kind of attention to things than I did before.

Music, for instance, the kind of music I usually ignore. Or

grouse about, feeling very curmudgeonly as I'm grousing. Whether I like it or not, the music of a car speeding through a sleeping neighborhood at three in the morning with the radio turned on full blast is now my music. I'm not getting the words yet, but listen hard enough, I will.

And wrestling. Two oiled half-naked men faking a hold and hitting the mat with a great bellow. What is the attraction? *Aargh,* they say and *hoomph* and *ohhh* as the oil and muscle and flab *thwocks* down, and what religious synapse is missing in me that I never knew there were people who worshiped here? I watch a lot of the kids rifle through these wrestling magazines. I never even knew they existed before.

Why don't I get it? What am I missing?

There are codes upon codes here. How can I figure them out?

How can I figure anything out?

News drifts in from the outside world. Sad news, a lot of it. A year ago, Amadou Diallo, an unarmed African immigrant, was shot forty-one times by four New York City policemen as he stood in the hallway of his Bronx apartment house. For the past month, the policemen were on trial for murder. And now the results are in: all four acquitted of all charges.

The day I hear that, I'm sure I'm not the only New Yorker who wonders if the city will explode.

But it doesn't. There are a few protests, but explosions, no. Maybe at other high schools around town, kids are angry, making speeches, planning demonstrations, but at the School of the New Millennium, beneath all the noise is an undertone of sullen silence. Does this mean the students don't care? Or do they care too much?

An uproar would be so much more comprehensible, and simply by being comprehensible, it would be a comfort. But my comfort is of no importance. The citizens of this country are sick of tourists. I'm on my own here. For though there is a guidebook for sale here, all the information in it is wrong.

So. No guide, no guidebook, a grueling travel schedule—tomorrow I pull into the town where they begin to love me, the day after that, the town where they love me more—and still I listen for bits of lingo I might recognize, customs that might remind me of a nation I have lived in before.

I am trying to understand. I mean really, honestly, without pretense. But how can I? It is hard enough to understand one person. How in the world can I begin to understand seventy-five?

I am contemplating the materials. All the things that might make my students who they are. Their families, their neighborhoods, the gossip they hear, the food they eat, or don't eat, the bruises they bear on their skins, or in memory. Never mind the most important, yet inexplicable thing, that innate voice, the *soul*. For I do believe in the soul, though sometimes, I forget.

Meanwhile, I wander around the halls, stranger in this never-never land of eternal youth where I was once at home. How weirdly natural it feels. For although this exact place feels new to me, it is still school, and with its halls and smell of buffed linoleum, it evokes that primal school feeling.

And while I do that, there's this girl I keep running into. I can't get away from her, as a matter of fact.

She is myself, of course. Who else? Far more real to me, at least here, than the adult self who replaced her. Any second now, it seems to me, my mother will be calling me to supper, and at my height of adolescent ungraciousness, I'll be snapping, *All right. I'm coming.*

The boys push, the girls push back, and Vincent Daly, 9A's class clown, heading out for an illicit cigarette, is heard to be saying: "When I grow up, man, I will never have a boring moment, not one, I'm going to *live*," and *bam*. There she is: plump, ungainly, prickly, secretly terrified, and even more secretly romantic. Oh, I should take her in hand, tell her to go to the gym and study harder for that math test, win friends and influence people, present her to my hairdresser, Monica the Hair Goddess, *why don't you do something with yourself for a change, stand up straight, stop moping?* But she's not interested in listening.

She pushes her long hair, her pride and joy, out of her eyes, before it flops back again. This is not what she planned. That she should run into me here, when I should so obviously be sitting in a café in Paris having witty repartee with a witty handsome French person, or snowshoeing up to the North Pole, hasn't she penciled in her agenda, *Tuesday, in the Year Whatever: Adventure. Glory. Art. Romance?*

"What," she gasps, "are you doing here?"

# The
# Fourteen
# Commandments

Sustained and directed effort can yield
high achievement for all students.

High minimum standards are set and all students'
curriculum is geared to these standards.

Knowledge and Thinking must be intimately
joined through the curriculum.

The school's small size encourages the development of strong
human bonds and discourages anonymity.

All students are heterogeneously grouped, which promotes
active tolerance and appreciation of differences.

The inclusion of special education students into all mainstream
classes also promotes tolerance, humility, and responsibility.

Staff members model practices that promote human rights. Staff members collaborate weekly in cluster planning meetings that are characterized by rich dialogue, discourse, and decision-making.

All students receive sensitivity training
about people with disabilities.

As future leaders in government, business, education, culture, and the community, our students are trained in peace education.

All students receive one-year training in Conflict
Resolution, Mediation, and Negotiation.

Students learn to value community, family, and service.

Every Child Has a Voice.

Every Child Is a Learner.

Thou Shalt Not Damage a Student's Self-Esteem.

I am sitting at my desk, watching Ricardo Silva reading *Goosebumps*.

It is early morning, during the fifteen minutes set aside when the entire high school engages in Silent Reading. Ordinarily I'd call this an oxymoron. Usually, it's so noisy that even Peter Garcia has admitted that the only book he will bring to school is *The Hobbit* because he knows it by heart anyway; he doesn't so much read it as let his eyes rest for a while on the familiar words.

But right now, there is quiet, there is reading. Today we have received a visit from Maria. If Nkruma is the king of the school, I think of Maria as one of those secret advisors and makers of policy that any government would think itself lucky to get. Her official title is aide, but what she really is, is librarian / office manager / patroller of the halls / enforcer. She doesn't want a grander title, she told me. As aide she enjoys an element of free agent, and she likes it that way.

Maria. How does she do it? She doesn't yell. She doesn't threaten. She never talks about self-esteem. But she's got It: *authority*. She's not big. She's not scary. But when she walks into the din of 9B and says, "Am I mistaken, but isn't this Silent Reading period?" a silence, if not the silence of reading, falls upon the room, and my students hang their heads.

"Yes," they say.

"So where are your books? Wilbur? Marcy? Pramila? I don't see any books."

"I don't have one."

"Coming to school without a book," she sighs. "And every morning starts with Silent Reading. You can go to the library, it's down the hall. Or you can go to the basket by Elizabeth's desk. The Parents Committee was kind enough to fill it with books. Well? What are you waiting for? Go and get one."

And this is when Ricardo Silva surprises me. He pulls *Goosebumps* out of his pocket. Slowly, slowly, his lips moving, he begins to read, a look of torment—is it the plot or the act of reading?—on his face.

*Goosebumps.* A book my friend's third-grader whizzed through. A third-grader with dyslexia, yet.

I don't know why Ricardo Silva is reading at a third-grade level. It could be that he's learning disabled. It could be that there's chaos or neglect at home. It could be that his mother drank or took drugs when he was in the womb, or that she is doing it now. It could be that he is drinking or taking drugs. It could be that he's beaten daily. It could be that nobody he knows reads anything, not even a newspaper. It could be that he has other things on his mind, like getting home in one piece. It could be that he cannot imagine a future. It could be that he's just no good at it. It could be that he doesn't give a damn. It could be all those things, or none, but whatever it is, I know this: I've entered pretty late in the game.

But there are people who concern me more than Ricardo Silva. Who baffle me, in a way that Ricardo does not. Take Stephen Thomas, for instance. He is a black boy with a look on his face of adult irony: remarkable, really. As he grows, his body, I'm sure, will change, but I cannot imagine his face changing, it already seems so grown-up and formed by thought and wit. He is a smart boy, he is—he cannot help it—a nice boy. I have seen him walk the streets by the School of the New Millennium quietly leading his little sister by the hand.

He comes to class and does nothing. He has been failing most of the year. He is never an instigator of trouble; but when things get out of hand his face lights up; he loves a bit of fun, a good giggle, and if that means summer school, what does he care?

Still, I suspect that if things were orderly, he might actually prefer working. And for that reason, and his intelligence, and for the fact that wild and hilarious he might be at times, but mean, never, I have my eye on Stephen Thomas.

This morning he is actually doing what he is supposed to do. He is sitting quietly, reading a book provided by the Parents Committee.

One eyebrow is raised, as if he were about to utter some cutting witticism at a cocktail party, something that will be quoted, among his acquaintances, for years.

Stephen is reading *The Bobbsey Twins*.

I'm sitting in my apartment the first week, turning the pages of the ninth-grade English textbook, a big blue shiny tome Leon acquired at April's request. This book is dedicated to one subject alone: writing. April was teaching one of the chapters on how to write your autobiography.

The easiest thing to do would just be to continue with this. But I don't want to have the students write their autobiographies. They are fourteen and fifteen years old, for Christ's sake. How much autobiography could most of them have acquired? Furthermore, aren't they tired of thinking about nothing but themselves? Isn't it my job to make their world bigger, not smaller? Not only that, didn't they write about their summer vacations and things like that back in the sixth grade?

I slam the book shut and murder a cockroach with it. Like most things having to do with this book, it is an act of overkill.

I know I'm being ungrateful, when many poor city schools have no recent textbooks at all, but I hate this book. This book, with its charts, its diagrams, its arrows, its use of jargon in boldface, even its very attractive worry-bead blue—a lucky color, but why do we need so much luck?—stinks of panic. April's likely panic, when she was yanked out of her dance classes and given a class in a subject she had never taught before. Leon's panic, when he saw April's panic, and yes, of course, he would get her something she could use, it would be all right, he promised. And most of all, the publishers' panic. It is obvious they have no idea why so many people have trouble writing, and what should be done about it. That's what all that typographical pizzazz says to me.

I, of course, have my own opinion, though no one's asking me. I am old-fashioned enough to believe people learn how to write through reading, reading a lot, reading all kinds of stuff, lowbrow, middlebrow, highbrow, brow once removed, it's all good, just plunge yourself into the printed page; there is no shortcut. And in this huge book, written, I'm sure, by people far more educated and knowledgeable than me, there are no reading passages longer than a page and a half. And dull passages, at that.

"Oh man," I announce to my cat, "give me a novel. A play. A book of short stories. Give me a real book."

The next day I go on a search for such a thing.

Maria unlocks the book room for me. It is kept stocked by the Parents Committee, which buys cheap books from a warehouse in Long Island.

By this time in the year whatever books were available have been ransacked, and this is what's left: Three copies of *To Kill a Mockingbird*. Five of *Jane Eyre*. Twenty-five of *Romeo and Juliet*. About a hundred of *The Call of the Wild*.

But I'm not ready to give up. When the school day is over I walk across the hall to visit Martin, the tenth- and eleventh-grade English teacher. He is an old pro—no chaos in his classroom. Pink, balding, a lover of corny jokes, he reigns in a room of exquisite neatness, the artifacts from his travels, the posters he has made on *Tragic Flaw* and *Conflict*, everything arranged just so.

"Do you realize," I say to Martin, "that these kids haven't read a book or a story all year?"

He shakes his head. " I wrote out an English curriculum for the ninth grade. For *all* the high school. Each year leading neatly into the next. There were plenty of books in that curriculum. I don't know why Leon doesn't want us to use it."

"A curriculum?" I feel like crying. "You wrote out a *curriculum?*"

"Come on. I'll introduce you to Rachel, the other high-school English teacher. Then we'll find you books."

Rachel is a stern-faced black woman with long satiny hair she pulls back in a bun. She, it turns out, is guarding one class set of ninth-grade English textbooks, a textbook with stories in it, and some pretty good stories at that.

"I'll lend them to you," she says.

It's not exactly perfect—there aren't enough copies for all my classes, so the students can't take them home, but at least there are real things to read in here written by real writers. "It's got to be better," I say, "when there are real books."


The next day I hand them out, and some students are glad. "At last, a book!" says Erica Reynolds, in 9A. I can barely hear her, though. The usual noise has already begun.

The din, of course, reaches its apotheosis in 9C. When Sammy Morales gets his book, he starts flipping through it, looking for something pornographic, and once he discovers that *The Story of O* was left out early in the selection process, he realizes that if you hold up your book and point to pictures, and laugh lewdly as if they *were* pornographic, they *become* pornographic. "Heh heh heh," he laughs, pointing to an alligator, and at the sight of an author, looking sensitive, he is almost on the floor. Most of the other boys join him.

It's not that some people don't want to read. A lot of them do. In 9A, I can't get the class settled enough to read silently, but I am able to subdue them by reading aloud, as if they were little children. But in 9B, and 9C, even that is impossible. Some of the students try to soldier on through the noise. They read. I don't know how much they understand, but they try. They try so hard, it kills me.

"Look," I say to Leon, this day, or the next, or the day after that, "whatever it is I'm doing, it's not working." It's probably foolish to confess my troubles to my boss, but I need help, and I'll take it from whatever quarter, and surely someone must know something is going on: the screams can be heard all the way down the hall.

Leon smiles, and since we are a family, let me say his smile is fatherly.

"They need a contract," he says. "They need to know exactly what is required of them. Here are some models of a contract. Write your own, have the parents sign it, and you'll see. They need to claim responsibility. Write a contract. Contracts work."

So I write one up. It doesn't even feel like *me* who is writing it. It's like I'm channeling some third-rate dictator of a tiny war-torn country, who never got the respect he knew was his due. It is a hideous thing. It makes me sick. All my anxiety and rage and terror of being fired and of not being fired is poured into it.

It's a pretty good contract. Bossy. Definite. Clear.

Intolerable.

"Excellent," says Leon, when I show him the contract. "This will work. You'll see. Now, reward yourself. Buy yourself a cappuccino."

# CONTRACT

Read the requirements below. Then sign on the provided line and bring it home for your parents or guardians to look over and sign, then return to me.

## Requirements and Grading Policy

In-class Writing: 30% of grade
Out-of-class Writing: 50% of grade
Class work, class participation, homework: 20% of grade

## Explanations

I will give an in-class writing exam every Friday (unless announced otherwise). These exams will be based on readings from the textbook *The Language of Literature*. Students will take notes and may use these while writing.

While taking an in-class exam, students may use a dictionary. Please write in blue or black pen and skip lines to make it legible. Pencil will not be acceptable.

In-class writings should be at least four paragraphs long. They should include an introduction, a conclusion, and at least two paragraphs explaining your point of view. They will be graded like this:

1. 25% for content
2. 25% for clarity and organization
3. 25% for development and language use
4. 25% for mechanics and grammar

In-class writings may not be rewritten for a better grade. If you miss the in-class on Friday, you will take it on the day you return. You may not leave class while taking an in-class writing. If you need water, air, etc., I suggest you get them before or after class.

Out-of-class writing will also be graded like the in-class writing: 25% for content, 25% for clarity and organization, 25% for development and language use, and 25% for mechanics and grammar. These compositions will be written three times. Each student will write a rough draft and second draft the first week a topic is introduced. The two drafts will be handed in, attached.

I will not correct the rough draft. This is for you to generate ideas. However, I will be happy to look at it and give you suggestions for ways to develop your ideas.

_____

Student's signature


_____

Parent or Guardian's signature

The next day I sit and watch as students like Ken and Sarah and Ahmed and Adam and Peter and Erica Reynolds slip their contracts into their knapsacks and others toss the contract onto the floor. And scream. And stomp on it. And tear it to pieces. And turn it into paper airplanes.

Is this the day I find a solution, a solution that unfortunately can only work once?

It is 9A, and I am looking at a blizzard of paper and kids banging their chairs around and howling. I stand up. This is the moment I am suppposed to say the words that will whip some into even greater frenzy: *Turn to page 92,* but it is too loud for me to even *think* 92, all I can think is *ohgodohgodohgodIcannot IcannotIcannotDothis,* and why am I bothering, why am I going through a single motion, and the pointlessness of this, of *anything,* overtakes me. "Oh," I say, and I rest my cheek on my hand, *I am so tired,* the weight of my skull, even without a real thought in it, is too much for me, *so tired,* that *Forget it,* I want to say, *Just . . . forget it,* that's what I'm going to say, really, that's what I begin to say, but somehow, somehow, that's not what I end up saying.

"Oh . . . *Fuck,*" I say.

Silence. Utter and complete. *Silence.*

*Fuck.*

You know what it's like, when you're holding a glass, and one second before it's going to drop, you think, *I'm going to drop this glass, I know it, it's going to fall, it's going to break,* and that is exactly what happens? You watch as the glass takes over. Slowly your hand unlooses, it can't help itself, and you simply become instrument for the end. So it is with Fuck. I become its passageway to the world. I feel it letter-by-letter slide out of me, as if this word had its own brain and body. *Oh wow. Lizzie,* I think, *you are going to say, No, you can't say, you can stop now, Yes, you are going to say, you can't stop now, No, Yes, gangway, here it comes, you press your teeth on the lower lip, good girl, now the burst, that's right: that little Anglo Saxon burst of exasperated air, and you've got it, sweetie, you've done it: fuck. Yes, fuck,* I am doing it, saying *fuck,* I am, I am, but I'm not, not me, not the me I once knew. *No.* I am merely the number-seven train taking fuck to where it has to go.

*Here.*

I am still resting my head on my hand. It feels as if I never will be able to lift it. I look out at the classroom.

*Fuck.* I hear that word a hundred times a day. Students say it without even thinking about it. And being here, even for a couple of weeks, I've said it a lot more often. Until now though, not when the kids are around.

*Fuck* still has power, I'm happy to report. Coming out of my mouth, anyway.

I can't think of another thing to say. Or do. I can't think of a way to pretend I didn't say fuck, or to give a speech, Leon-style, about how even leaders of today sometimes lose control. How can I give any kind of speech when my cheek is still glued to my hand?

No. I stare at my class and they stare back, and *Fuck* settles in like a new student. The one who has been kicked out of Bryant High School and Newtown and Louis Armstrong and is now ready to become a Leader of Tomorrow. *Fuck* takes up a lot of room.

I am looking at them looking at me, and *I don't care, I don't care, Fire me, go ahead, do me a favor, fire me,* that's what most of my brain is thinking, but not even defiant, just weary. Just accepting the foregone conclusion.

The other part of my brain is thinking, *rent.*

I have never seen those children look so much like children: scared. Oh, they wanted to drive me to the edge, they just didn't want me to go over it. They wanted me angry. They wanted me humiliated. They didn't want me defeated.

It's ugly to see an adult, defeated.

How long does this last?

Silence has a way of expanding. Minutes? Hours? Years? Probably a minute. Maybe two. But they are not bad minutes. For while they are going on, we are tired and miserable together.

Then Nestor pipes up. He surprises me.

"Don't worry, Miss," he says. "We won't tell nobody."

If only they would.

On the number-seven train, I actually *read* my contract.

"Damn," I say, appalled. "This is a lot of work."

Then I open up *The Village Voice* and check my horoscope.

Transformative experiences are coming my way.

As I'm walking to work, I pass Park Sang, one of the high-school science teachers, skulking in a fenced-off little yard in front of an apartment house, smoking a cigarette. It's a cool, dank day, and he's shivering.

"Hey," I say.

He gives me a conspiratorial smile, and proceeds with his important business, which is smoking.

It's a dog's life, being a role model.

Even as I am slowing my pace, the white block of the School of the New Millennium coming into view, I know there are people out there piercing their nipples and drinking too much, falling in love with all the wrong people or even the right ones, putting on tight leather pants or false eyelashes, dancing all night in a dive somewhere, cheating on their husbands with other husbands' wives. Yes, even as I am rubbing my coat of stray cat hairs, I long for the bigger world, its infinite promise for splendor and mistake, for mess and all its consequences. Why can't Park Sang smoke his cigarette in comfort, proudly, so everyone can see? Is it really such a sin to have a bad habit? It hardly seems fair, when the air by the doors of the school is thick with smoke from the students' Marlboros.

There's a problem with this role model business.

A role model is supposed to set a good example, a role model is supposed to inspire. But look at Park Sang, unable to stand up and announce, *Damn straight I have a bad habit. And you. You have only good ones?* And look at me: miserable, harried, dodging my creditors, covered with hairs from a different species. Look at any of us, marking papers, calling up parents, required to exercise hour upon hour of egoless empathy.

What kid in his right mind would want to be us?

One day, on the way home, I find myself on the number-seven train, sitting next to Calvin, the math teacher.

"You get too excited, Elizabeth," he says. "You've got to calm down."

"And how do I do that?" I say.

"You just calm down. Otherwise, you never leave the job. It's with you all the time. It drives you crazy." Then he pauses. "Of course, that's what it was like for me, the first two years. For two years, I took this job home every night. That's all I thought about. I had trouble," he confesses, "with my *authority.*"

I am looking at Calvin, curiously.

*Math teacher:* foreign creature. His room hung with signs proclaiming DO NOT CROSS THE LINE OF SYMMETRY and MATH: MADE FROM THE BEST STUFF ON EARTH. I could point out, of course, that he needs letters to get his idea across, but why argue? It is pleasant to think he likes it so much.

Calvin has an accent.

Perhaps it is an accent from Algebraland.

"Do you mind me asking where you're from?" I say.

"Vietnam," he says.

Now I am looking at Calvin *really* curiously. I have a million questions to ask, and as any math teacher will tell you, in the time allotted us there is no way I can even get to a fraction of them.

How old is he? Thirtyish, I guess. A thin man, in jeans, with the ascetic mournful look of a medieval saint. His eyes give away nothing.

"Do you remember the war?" I say.

"Of course I do."

"Where were you?"

"Saigon."

It's hard work, interrogating a math teacher.

"What was it like?" I say.

"What was it like?" he replies. "We ran from one side of the street and then to the other."

I am sitting in Martin's room, after school ends, probably making a complete nuisance of myself, watching him slide things into folders and stack and put away, hoping, I suppose, that some of his talent for order will rub off on me.

Is Martin my role model?

This room is so clean I half suspect that after the custodian has done his job Martin sneaks back to give the floor an extra wipe and polish. His classes have been planned, he told me, day by day, all the way up to June. Handouts are sitting in their folders waiting to be given out on their designated date. It is a relief to sit in a room so shining, the absolute antithesis of soda and gum.

And besides, he is not only neat, he has the Gift: I have seen him in action, and I know. He walks through the halls smiling, radiating a Shakespearean monkish goodwill, always ready, it seems, to give advice or comfort or tell a corny joke. I have seen children come up to him, the same children who had just been insulting me, *Oh Martin,* they say, *Hi, Martin, Martin, Martin,* and he beams upon them. In class I have seen him hold forth theatrically, while his students, rapt, do not make a sound. They hold their faces up, and drink him in.

Once I thought I had a little bit of a Gift. Now I know I was wrong. I could merely finagle someone who wanted to do it anyway into doing what he wanted to do. But that was not the Gift. That was merely a cheap talent for mutual seduction. It was not the spiritual and selfless act of a leader who could give and give without longing for reward.

*Oh. I am bad. I am very, very, bad.*

"Why did you leave the monastery?" I ask him.

"It was the sixties," he says, and makes a face. "Suddenly they wanted to modernize. Suddenly it was like every place else."

Then I realize: He's right. Robes, funny haircuts, sandals, beads, chanting, candles, incense, communal living: it *was* like every place else, back then.

"So, what did you do next?" I say.

"Played piano in a flamenco bar."

Is Martin my role model?

How could he be?


Perhaps *Rachel* is my role model. Who wouldn't want a little bit, or a version, anyway, of what she's got? The intelligent and kindly husband, the brilliant and confident children, the apartment with the view of the Hudson, the summer house, and most of all, her pleasure in these things? It would be *A-OK*, I think, to be a little bit settled, instead of constantly caught up in the act of becoming, because I don't want to think—*I cannot think*—that I have simply become.

Rachel is sitting in her room, pissed off.

She's angry about the Amadou Diallo verdict. "Innocent," she fumes. "An unarmed man shot *forty-one* times and the jury declared those cops *innocent?*"

"The prosecution played down the race issue," I say. "That was their mistake. They hardly mentioned—I don't even *know* if they mentioned—race."

"But it *is* a race issue."

"I know."

She glares at me, as if I really didn't know, or even worse, had been on the jury. Ordinarily I find such assumption irritating, but given the circumstances, I let it pass.

"Do you know," she says, "every time my son goes out of the house at night I don't know if he's going to come back? I have to let him go, of course. But he could have been the one in that doorway." She looks down at the pile of papers before her and frowns.


*Teachers' Room.*

Calvin is lying on the couch in a state of frail exhaustion. His delicate bones, his old jeans, his arm thrown across his eyes: nobody does frail exhaustion better than Calvin.

"Oh," he moans. "Leon is ridiculous. He makes us do things that are *ridiculous*. Like the time with the cops?"

"Oooh," I say, brightening. "Cops? Tell me."

"I prefer to forget," he sighs.

"Maybe it's because you are a cop," I say.

He laughs. He has a great laugh, a laugh that embodies all the rage he usually tries to repress.

"You have a devil laugh," I say.

"And who are you?" he asks, half sitting up and looking around the room. "Demons?"

Knock on the glass door. No one gets up to answer it. Calvin sinks back into the couch. The knocking continues until someone finally stands up and attends to it. Nkruma walks in.

"What is it?" he snaps. "You see a black face, you think it's a student?"

Pointless to say there are quite a few black teachers, and that same thing happened to me last week. Instead I cut to the chase.

"No. We're just too lazy to answer the door."

"I couldn't find my key," he says, pacing. "Why do we have to have a key?"

"You know why. Keep the students out."

"Bathroom key opens the teachers' lounge," says Vivian. "That's what you need to remember. Bathroom key."

At the main table, the table where teachers eat their lunch or prepare their lesson plans, Louis and Park Sang are having a spirited conversation.

"What kind of school *is* this? I know we're supposed to be developing leaders, but what *kind* of leaders? And how are we supposed to be doing that?"

"Listen." Louis lowers his voice, confidentially. "How's the science they do with you?"

Park Sang laughs. "Terrible. I mean, not all of them. But mainly . . . *terrible*. How's the science they do with you?"

"Terrible."

"So it's not a science school."

"No. I wouldn't call it a science school."

"It's not a math school," Calvin intones from his couch.

"It's not a global studies school."

"It's certainly not an English school," I snap.

"It's an arts school," Park Sang decides. "Everybody takes art classes, and we've got the drama teacher, and we've got more than one music teacher . . . it's an arts school. That's what we have to remember. A performing arts school."

"But what about dance?" somebody says. "They made April give it up and teach English."

"For a while," I say.

A gloom falls upon the denizens of the Teachers' Room.

march²
**everybody's got a voice**

# LITTLE THINGS

Most of us miss out
on life's big prizes.
The Pulitzer.
The Nobel.
Oscars.
Emmys.
But we're all
eligible for life's
small pleasures.
A pat on the back.
A kiss behind the ear.
A four-pound bass.
A full moon.
An empty parking space.
A crackling fire.
A great meal.
A glorious sunset.
Hot soup.
Cold beer.
Don't fret about copping
life's grand awards.
Enjoy its tiny delights.
There are plenty for all of us.

—Sign in the School of the New Millennium office

Peace.

No Walkmans, no hats, no cans of soda.

Peace . . . and quiet.

Let me tell you about silence, that secret buried in the inner ear. It has a dull burnish to it, a softness, like a good room you could live in for a long time. Inside it, I feel the bones in my head settle back into their assigned places. And it feels good. They are happy to be there, back where they belong.

The old proverbs are right. They almost always are. This is what gold would sound like if it had a sound, not hard and shiny but like the thin leaves pressed into the ceilings of domes.

It is nine in the morning, and there is a pleasant, sleepy hush in the gymnasium. Outside the windows the neighborhood lazily rouses itself. Rolling its babies in its carriages. Looking for bargains in the boxes of shirts and flashlights set out on the sidewalks. Sitting in the cafes and studying the racing form.

And here, in the soft gray light, peace.

A coffee urn gushes. The juice of oranges flows out of pitchers. Bagels practically halve themselves and offer up their tender flesh for us.

Teacher Development Day.

Who knew three little words could have such meaning?

Forget *I love you*. This is special. This is the day different from all other days. The day when teachers come to school to work on their development while Sammy Morales . . . well, Sammy Morales gets to stay home and work on his hormones.

It is beautiful, Teacher Development Day.

Much, much better than a four-pound bass or a parking space.

Even better than a four-pound bass lying *inside* a parking space.

It is Heaven.

I admit my sights are sinking lower and lower. Once I thought Heaven would be (if I believed in such things; and of course, I do not) angels, Mozart, pomegranates, orgasm with no morning after. Now I think it's any room with *them* not in it.

What a thing to think, but I'm drinking my coffee, and I can't pretend to myself I'm not thinking it: No Them = Bliss.

*Oh Lizzie. Listen to you. That bitterness.*

It is the voice of the madwoman on the subway, clutching her pocketbook too tightly and accusing, accusing them all.

*How about a little compassion, Liz Dear? Can't you think, broken homes, hormones, the media with its terrible pressure to have sex and be thin?*

*Is this the voice you want in your head?*

So old. Cold. Resentful.

*Envious . . .*

Wouldn't I like to be working on *my* hormones, polishing them up till they gleam like nickel, loving that shine, the swiftness and unpredictability of my own body, wouldn't I like the thrill of the first ride?

Sure I would.

When I was fifteen, did I think Heaven would be like this?

A sleepy good morning to Miriam and Martin, no papers to shuffle. A glass of orange juice?

"Okay, okay, everybody, settle down," says Leon, standing up and putting his hands on what would be his waist if he had one. He's beaming. He likes this kind of thing. The discussion of theory. The tossing around of big dreams of what can be done. "We've got a lot to do today. The New Millennium has *entered* the New Millennium, and we've got to be ready for it. Okay? Settle down, settle down, but first—"

First we need to break down our inhibitions.

A terrifying thought, for if I broke down mine, I don't know what I would do, but it wouldn't be pretty.

Never mind. Inhibitions are meant to be broken down, like jalopies.

And here we have a member of the Theatre of the Oppressed to help us do it.

"Hey, everybody," he says, giving a friendly wave.

Does anyone else see the comedy in this? Or am I so barnacled over in cynicism I am the only one? As far as I'm concerned, every *day* in Room 313 is the Theatre of the Oppressed, and I don't need any experts to show me the way.

Still. Nice to know that when the School of the New Millennium is lucky enough to get itself a nice fat arts grant, it spends some of its money, anyway, on reinforcing my curriculum.

We're studying *The Bacchae* from the inside out. Groping our way toward text.

"Link hands," we're told. "It *works!*"

How obedient we are. It is an obedience we would never ask of our students. We link, and then, as he directs us to do, we start going round and round the room, under each other's arms, never letting go of the hands, that's the point, never breaking the connection. It's a cross between Twister and a Balkan folk dance, but no music: just the sound of inhibitions breaking down.

And now they *are*. Bit by bit I feel them all drop away: the hate, the lies, the paranoia: in a minute or two I would trust Miriam with my *life*.

We're all naked now, truly naked, mud-stained, fucking into primal consciousness, sobbing with the first memory of clawing our way down the birth canal, in a few minutes we're *close*.

And then it's over.

Well, not quite.

We're still standing in a circle, holding hands, sheepish and relieved that it had gotten no more embarrassing than this.

"Let go of your hands," we're told. "How are you feeling?"

"Sweaty," mumbles Calvin.

Then we all start waddling off again to the buffet table. But Leon is shouting: "Okay, okay, no time to waste! Into your clusters! We've got a lot to do today! We're going to make *change* happen! And you know how it happens! First, there's the *storming*. Then there's the *forming*. Then there's the *norming*. And then the *performing*. So let's go! Let's start *storming!*"

I march off with the high-school humanities cluster. Martin, Rachel, Miriam, Nkruma, Tom, and myself settle into our assigned classroom, and we start talking in a halfhearted way about all the wonderful things we're going to do in the future, but fifteen or so minutes in Nkruma slams his hands down on the table.

"This is just crap," he says.


The high-school humanities cluster suddenly sits up, wipes the sleep out of its eyes.

"Forget this," he says. "Just forget this. We can't do this, any of this, we're just fooling ourselves, if we can't talk about our *real* problem, which is *discipline*.

"I'm not saying this for myself," he continues, Nkruma, the King of the School, the *cool* teacher, the role model for us role models, "They listen to *me*. But some of our kids, they can't handle this. They just can't. They need discipline. They need form. They need to be told exactly *what* they are supposed to do. They need to know there are real consequences. Not having their lunch card pulled. Real consequences. I'm telling you. I know. *I* was one of those kids. I couldn't have survived a place like this. This is not a place for everybody, and we have to stop pretending that it is. Because if we can't get rid of the kids who don't belong, this place isn't going to survive either."

"*We're* not going to survive!" someone yells.

"If some of those kids talked on the street the way they talk to me," says Miriam, "they would be dead."

"We need a guidance counselor! We don't even have a guidance counselor!"

"How about a masseuse?"

"And a full-time psychologist!"

"For *us!*" snaps Miriam.

## the doctrine
## according to nkruma

That morning we spend very little time talking about our future, glorious though it might be. We talk about the present, the relentlessness of each day piling upon the next.

Some of it is just griping. I see that. But it is necessary griping. For this is how I step out of the isolation of my classroom, and understand that what is happening is not happening only to me, but to others as well.

It's true, I have my own particular reasons for failing. I am, after all, a kind of permanent sub, and I know what kids do to subs. I've never taught high school before, and it probably is the wrong job for me in the first place. But I am not the only one who feels like things are out of control.

Why? It's a good question. I look around the room, and these are not the teachers of tabloid myths: illiterate, sex-harassing monsters who are bleeding the system for whatever they can get. Far from it.

There's Martin, product of parochial schools and the monastery, lover of Shakespeare and corny jokes, who brings into the classroom—I have watched him—a little, perhaps, of the flamenco bar, that color and flair, that comical sense of theater. Nkruma, our firebrand, sitting on the edge of his desk in his classroom decorated with bolts of kente cloth and portraits of Frederick Douglass and Karl Marx, talking to the kids in that way he has—a passionate oratory with an intimate tinge, the key to his star power. There's Rachel, raised in Greenwich Village and Martha's Vineyard, a proud member of the black bourgeoisie, a woman whose children received riding lessons, language lessons, piano lessons, a woman with a vague air of superiority to many around her, but I forgive her for it, for she is so kind. There's Miriam, whose slightly Victorian formality reveals her Caribbean roots, and Tom, the hardworking suburban boy.

In some ways they are very different, but in essential ways, the same. These are smart people, dedicated people, people, I now see, who often go home in despair. It's terrible to be around chaos all the time.

Round and round they go, talking about school policy, their attempts to go along with it, and the oppressive weight of their failures. I listen closely, because I know we will never have, the lot of us, a conversation quite like this one. Only Nkruma, with his competence, and his confidence, and his glamorous aura, could free us to confess our dirty little secrets. Because it feels dirty, at least here, to have doubts. It's against the school's whole philosophy, and without the philosophy, what is this place? Nothing.

When there's a pause in the conversation, I start asking the questions I've been dying to ask. I want to know about the school's history; not the history of the promotional flyer, but its true history, and what it is we are supposed to be doing here.

"The way I look at it," says Nkruma, "there are five kinds of kids in this school. There are the True Believers' kids—the ones whose parents are involved in the philosophy and the running of this place. Some of those kids have been with us since the beginning. There are the ordinary neighborhood kids, kids whose parents just want them to go to the local school. There are kids who live near a bad school, so their parents send them across town to this one. Then, because this place is small, it has a reputation as a place that gives a lot of individual attention, so we get a lot of kids with mild learning disabilities. That's group four. But we also get kids with big learning disabilities, *huge* behavior problems, kids who have already flunked out or been kicked out of a few schools, and guess what—*we're* not doing that well with them either."

"There are kids in my class who are reading and writing on a fifth-grade level," says Martin. "If that. Mixed in with kids at the tenth- and eleventh-grade level. How can I teach both at the same time? I wish Leon could see that."

"I think Leon does see that," says Tom. "But we don't really have a choice. The Board of Ed didn't want us to be elitist. Some magnet schools select students by exam and interview. We can't. We have a quota of local kids, and kids whose parents were involved with the founding of the school—we have some leeway there—but for the rest—it's the lottery system. And if we go charter, it'll be even worse. We'll have to select students *only* by lottery. That's what the Board of Ed told us. That's the price of our freedom, I guess. If we want to break away from the Board of Ed—from all that bureaucracy, all those controls—because that's what it means, this charter business, right? We take their money, but *we* decide what to do with it—well, if we do it, we have to take anyone who comes along, but the problem with that is, we don't have the facilities to deal with every student that comes along. I mean, on paper we do, but in reality?"

"Why not?" I burst out.

"Okay," says Tom. "Let's take one example. *Inclusion.* Hordes of kids with learning and behavior problems used to be dumped into special ed classes. Often those classes ended up being ghettos for kids who, with work and attention, could do more—in other words, some of those kids were not really special ed at all. They were classified as that because no one knew what to do with them. So now we have a new idea: include kids with learning and behavior problems in regular classes, because they have a *right* to an equal education. Or what passes as an equal education. And we do rescue a few kids that way, and I'm glad about that. But for the rest? Just because we change the rules, doesn't mean we change a problem. All we do is change the *locale* of the problem."

"I would say I ignore about twenty percent of my class," says Martin. "Maybe more. I never really counted. All I know is, there are students I'm just not able to reach, if I want to reach all the others."

"You?" I say. "*You?* I thought we were supposed to teach everybody."

"Nobody can teach everybody," Nkruma says. "A lot of these kids have enormous problems. I do what I can. But there's only one of us in the classroom. There are twenty-five of them. I'm sure Leon is right. Kids need individual attention, perfectly tailored to suit them. But how, logistically, can you give individual attention to twenty-five people at once?"

"We shouldn't even be talking about this at all," says Rachel. "We're supposed to be doing group teaching. We're supposed to be figuring out what our students are supposed to learn, and how we're going to get them there. You know how much better things would be if I knew what students had learned the year before, and where they're supposed to be going? This is the core of learning. And if we can't do it ourselves, we should hire someone to help us. I've asked Leon to get a curriculum specialist. There are some good ones around, I hear. But every time I ask him, he just brushes me off."

"I think we can't think about curriculum," says Martin. "Not really. Remember? He threw out mine. I think there's a reason. If we had a challenging curriculum, a lot of kids would fail. And then start listening to people complain!"

"Still," says Miriam. "A lot might pass. A lot of those kids are smarter than they think, if we just gave them a chance."

"True," adds Rachel. "A lot of them have been told their whole lives how dumb they are. By their families. By the world. How cool it is to act dumb. How there's nothing smarter than acting dumb. We could change that, if we had a chance."

"We have to figure out who we are," says Nkruma. "Are we a school where students come to get challenged? That means that we discipline kids who try and stop that from happening. Because some will. Some always will. Or, we could just be a place where students feel *good* about themselves, no matter what. If that means lying, okay, we lie. Not that most of the kids believe us. Not that they should."


When the humanities cluster slinks back, later that afternoon, to report on our discussion, we must look like terrible spoilsports.

Every other cluster seems to have spent the morning discussing this grant they are going to apply for, this or that project the students will attempt, and the wonderful prizes they will win. And us?

"Uh," says Martin, "we discussed discipline."

You know that feeling you get, when you are at a formal dinner party, and somebody makes a gaffe? Nobody knows how to respond, so nobody does. People just wait for the silence to exhaust itself, so they can pretend nothing happened, and then begin again. You know the heaviness of that silence? That is the heaviness in the room, after Martin says "discipline."

Finally Leon says, "Thanks, teachers! Inspiring work! But we don't have time for more discussion if we want to see this video." He dims the lights. "It's a great one. We saw it last year, but it was so good, I thought I would show it again."

I can see why Leon likes it. On the screen, a man in a good suit tells his followers—a gaggle of genteel ladies in sexless dresses and wooden beads—that every child deserves individual attention, individually designed tests if necessary, individually given and individually graded. Rather than putting up a fight—who has the time to design individual tests for individual students, and how would it then be considered a test?—the ladies respond the way I'm sure Leon dreams people should respond. They gasp at every *bon mot* that slips from the lecturer's lips.

I find myself sighing, the way I used to do as a high-school student, when things got too dull or insulting. Then I look around in the dark, and I see Miriam with her arms crossed primly across her chest, and Martin, who is gazing transfixed at something out the window, and as for Nkruma—he slides all the way down in his chair and rolls his eyes up in disgust. It takes all the energy he's got not to bolt.

# MIDDLE AND HIGH SCHOOL STUDENTS!

## Free Food!! Free Fun!!

*Make your* PARENTS
*do some homework for a change!!*

THE NM PTA AND OUR ANNENBERG PARTNERSHIP PRESENTS

# "I'm Speaking, But You're Not Listening"

A FREE 2-day communication and conflict resolution workshop for Parents and Guardians, given by the THEATRE OF THE OPPRESSED LABORATORY

Come share, learn, and problem-solve as we explore the difficulties of communicating in families, using fun and engaging theatre games and techniques. See how art can be used to enrich your family, your life, and the life of your child.

NO THEATRE EXPERIENCE NECESSARY

Saturday morning, the phone rings.

"I have good news," says Leon.

*Sammy Morales was run over by a bus.*

"Yes?" I say.

"Your fingerprints have been cleared. They rushed it through for me. Now you can be paid. It took just a few weeks, Elizabeth. That's not so bad, is it?"

"No," I say. "Not so bad."


Saturday morning, the phone rings again.

It's the Census Bureau. In the throes of semi-employment, I had taken their test, I had put the *m* before *n* and 7.53 before 7.6, I had finished in record time. And now they want me. They've never seen such alphabetizing.

They're offering me the highest position they've got, group leader.

"Let me think about it," I say.

Am I out of my mind? No benefits, no vacation, strictly temporary, and I can't imagine this is glamorous work. I can't think it would be fun. Still. Would I be telling someone to take his hat off, or not to drink his soda? *Excuse me, madam, take the gum out of your mouth, and tell me honestly, for everyone has a voice: how many people live in your place of residence?*

So I am thinking about it. I'm taking the number-seven train in, standing at the window and looking down at the populace waiting to be counted, and suddenly alphabetizing sounds pretty darn good to me: it is a skill, it is good work, to fix the *j* before the *k*, not everyone can do it. Obviously. Amazing, how *anybody* wanting you gives you power. Or the delusion of power. The Census Bureau wants me. They want me a lot. *Take that, take that, you ungrateful lackeys of the School of the New Millennium.*

I have uncovered, in the book room, one class set of *Romeo and Juliet.*

Just one, so the kids can't take their books home and read them, but it's something. If I weren't feeling so incompetent, maybe I could give a real class about something worth teaching. But I walk into 9B, and hand out the books, and open my mouth, and the sheer pointlessness of it overwhelms me. Nothing comes out.

Nothing *can* come out.

Is this what it was like for April?

And whatever happened, really happened, to April? Where is she now, and how is she doing, and is there any hope for recovery? Suddenly, I need to know.

Tom and Nkruma are spelling me more and more. When the noise gets too loud one or the other sticks his head in the door and tells me to take a break, and even as I'm leaving, to sit for a minute in the hall, I hear him appeal to the students' sense of discipline, their kindness, their good sense, *something.*

Not that it works. Not that it ever works. Things quiet down when Tom or Nkruma are speaking, but the minute I walk into the classroom, the noise begins again.

One day, Nkruma is lecturing, and I am sitting in the hall on one of the sofas next to Tom, and I'm embarrassed as hell, just a worm in the face of his youth and competence, I'm pathetic, my whole life, my poverty, my great ambitions, my loneliness, my old jeans, my coat with its cat hair, my complete inability to control a group of fifteen-year-olds, my way-too-easy welling up of tears, I'm just completely pathetic, I'm a loser, man. I just happen to be a loser with a job offer.

"You know," I say, "I've been offered a job somewhere else, and I'm thinking of taking it."

Tom's face changes, and I suddenly understand the obvious: *They do not want me to leave.*

Yes, they know it's chaos in there. There's screaming and crying and hitting and God knows what all, and some of that screaming and crying emanates from me, but it is March, and I am the fourth teacher in there, and frankly, I could smear my body with excrement and start speaking in tongues and at least until June, anyway, they would do anything to keep me. Anything.

This is when I start to go under, this is when I allow my fear to take over. *Be a general,* I tell myself, but all I can think of is the six hundred riding into the Valley of Death.

I don't want to be a general. I am not a military kind of girl.

I refuse to be a general.

I simply *can't* be a general.

I am standing outside Room 313, trembling. Rachel, on her way to her own class, sees me, looks into my face, takes me by the shoulders, and says:

"Oh you poor dear."

I start sniffing.

"You should have told me it was like this," she says. "I'll help you, whatever you need, don't worry, we'll get you through this," and I start to cry.

"I can't go in there," I say. "They've got me beat."

Now Judy bustles up. She is the assistant principal, transferred recently, I gather, from another school, a more traditional one, and she still has a little of the cozy domestic air of places gleaming with lemon wax, where the Pledge of Allegiance is recited every day.

"Come on," she says, "into my office, quick."

She sits me down and hands me a box of tissues. "I know what you need. I'm going to get it for you. So I have to leave for a minute, but don't worry. I'm locking the door. Nobody will be able to get in. You just sit here, Elizabeth, will you be okay?"

I nod meekly.

Judy disappears, and in ten minutes she's back:

"Sugar is what you need," she says, handing me a *cafe con leche* and a guava pastry.

Sugar *is* what I need. Lots and lots of sugar. Gleaming granules of sweetness and light.

God, I'm getting fat, I'm beginning not to fit into any of my clothes and I'm too poor to buy new ones. But who cares if I have thighs the size of Roosevelt Boulevard? This is medicine I'm taking.

"Eat up," Judy says, and starts eating up herself.

"I should be on a diet," she confides, licking her fingers. "My daughter's wedding, you know . . ."

I would love to chat all day about her daughter's wedding, but then Leon shows up.

"Be a general," he says.

"I can't be a general."

"Come, Elizabeth."

"I can't."

"Give it a try," he says, gently. "Come on. You can do it."

"No I can't."

"Yes you can."

"No I *can't.*"

But I do realize I can't sit here forever, so I blow my nose and stumble into class, and one of the nicer girls says to me, "Where were you?"

"In Judy's office, having a nervous breakdown," I quip, and she looks so sick it occurs to me that she's actually seen a teacher have a nervous breakdown. Maybe it was pretty distressing to watch. Maybe my little joke will have long-reaching and horrific effects. Ruin 'em for life.

But what do I care if I have destroyed young lives? In an office somewhere in midtown Manhattan, there's a whole lot of alphabetizing to do. I just have to say yes, and I'll be doing it. To hell with *Romeo and Juliet.* How can a dagger and a moonlit night compare with the importance of New York State getting properly counted? This is congressional representation we're talking about.

"Here's the play," I say. "Why don't we just take turns reading it out loud?"

My lesson. I sit there, they read out loud, or at least some of them do, and if they understand a word they're reading, or not, is of no importance. What's important is that I'm not fleeing the room. What more can you ask from the educational system?

When I stumble out that afternoon, Alex, the music teacher, is sitting outside the school in a folding chair, sunning himself. He

would be attractive enough if he didn't spend half his time looking as if he were posing for Edvard Munch's *The Scream*. But today
he seems strangely relaxed. Could it be drugs, and where did he
get them?

"Burnt out already?" he says. "When I can't cope, I show a
movie. Sometimes I show a few movies a week. Hell, I'd show
movies five days a week if I could."

Okay, why not? I'll become the kind of teacher I used to mock
who sits there in the dark, taking deep breaths—*could she be sleeping?*—while the movie rolls.

Thank you, Alex. I go to the video store, and I pick up the lavish sixties *Romeo and Juliet,* the one with the lavish Renaissance
costumes and lovers too pretty to live. Is there nudity in it? There
might be, but only for a minute, I think. There's nudity in almost
everything. At least no one could argue with the educational
value of Shakespeare and I do believe that nowhere in the movie
is there one exploding head. But even before I slip it into the VCR,
more help arrives.

Natalie.

Who was the one who decided I couldn't go it alone, but I
couldn't go either? Whoever it is, I'm grateful. For here she is.
*Natalie.*

She is a parent of one of the elementary school students. She
is also the substitute who took over the ninth grade when April
collapsed, and now she's back. Ostensibly, to give me assistance
and encouragement. But really, to make sure I don't run out of
the room.

"Hi," I breathe. How pleasant to have one person in the room
with whom I can have a fragment of a conversation.

I slip the video in and without any attempt at explanation turn off the lights, and the students take up their places. A few are rapt. A few listen, or try to. Others, after a while, are unable to concentrate—the actors talk so funny, move so slow. The movies they're used to are so much louder and aggressive. Kids begin talking again. Eating their Doritos, licking their lollipops, the new kind that just came out, the ones in the plastic holder shaped like a switchblade. Just open it with a snap of the wrist and you're ready to lick. Tim'n'Bob are punching each other. Some of the girls are gossiping—but not softly, or surreptitiously; the idea is to do it as obviously as possible. Cindy Fernandez is among them, but when she wants to watch the movie, she screams: "SHUT UP! I CAN'T HEAR! I WANT TO WATCH THE *MOVIE*. JUST SHUT THE FUCK UP, WILL YOU?"

A boy sprawls across the tables, and commences his nap.

And Natalie sits there, doing what really is a full-time task. She's filling in misbehavior cards. The ones that get your outside lunch privileges taken away.

"Check," Natalie murmurs, looking around the room, "check, check, check, check."

"SHUT UP SHUT UP SHUT UP SHUT UP SHUT THE FUCK UP."

"If these are the future leaders of New York," I say to Natalie, "I'm moving."

STUDENT BEHAVIOR REPORT

FOR_____/_____/00_____

Student:_____Class:_____

Late_____Awol_____Left room without permission_____

Eating_____Drinking_____Walkmans_____Hats_____

Talking_____Abusive Language_____

Hitting, other violent behavior_____Disruptive behavior_____

No Homework_____Unprepared_____Other_____

Student:_____Class:_____

Late_____Awol_____Left room without permission_____

Eating_____Drinking_____Walkmans_____Hats_____

Talking_____Abusive Language_____

Hitting, other violent behavior_____Disruptive behavior_____

No Homework_____Unprepared_____Other_____

Student:_____Class:_____

Late_____Awol_____Left room without permission_____

Eating_____Drinking_____Walkmans_____Hats_____

Talking_____Abusive Language_____

Hitting, other violent behavior_____Disruptive behavior_____

No Homework_____Unprepared_____Other_____

Zen, I think. Zen. I'm not exactly sure what Zen is—I've never read seriously about it, or been to Zen practice—but it's in the air, at least my air, anyway. Zen detachment, I think. Let each thing be itself, no need to interfere. Let each thing in its essence *be* its essence. This is how it works:

"Miss," a student says, a holdover from the old days, something he cannot shake, something he'd rather call me, and I prefer Miss, too, it creates a pleasant distance between us—truth is, neither of us wants to get that close—"Can I go to the bathroom?"

"Sure," I say. "Cool. Take as long as you like. One hour, two hours. How about some reading material?"

He looks at me, uneasy. "The other teachers tell me to get back as soon as possible. In case I miss something."

I shrug and give him my best *What the hell* smile.

Zen is good. Zen is transforming the typhoon inside me into a smooth black stone I swallowed. Serene, serene. Zen is going to help me survive until summer vacation. Because although I know I should feel no desire, I am so worldly I desire my summer vacation. It is one thing the census job can't offer me. I desire my summer vacation very much.

*HOMO. HOMO. HOMO.*

Zen.

*LET'S SEE WHO HAS THE STRONGEST ASS IN THIS ROOM.*

Zen.

*RICARDO. RICARDO. STOP PUNCHING MY FUCKING TIT.*

Natalie is resorting to the old method, the Western method of recording and reporting bad behavior. And I say, let her. Let Natalie be Natalie. Writing it down. Handing it in. To do this is to somehow be more of herself, more Natalie.

In the short time I practice, those few days when "Cool" is the word that emerges most often out of my mouth, Zen fails me twice.

The first time, it's with Gibran. He is a sullen boy from Guyana, one of those quiet, glowering boys steeped in the life of refusal: he will not do what asked to do, is all, he will write his name down, but don't ask for anything more. It is enough, he seems to say, without saying anything. And now he's running up to me, laughing, with Tim'n'Bob, the wrestling, punching, hooting, beating-head-against-locker-duo right behind him, looking over his shoulder and repeating their favorite mantra: *grossgrossgross.* "Look," says Gibran.

He has driven a pushpin deep into the web of skin that separates his thumb from his forefinger.

"Cool," I say.

Yes, that's what I say. *Cool.*

By the end of the day, he is suspended for trying to drive that pushpin deep into other people's hands. And other parts as well, I gather. "Has he been acting strangely lately?" asks Judy.

"Well," I say, feeling the slippage, the limits of cool.

The second time is more embarrassing.

For a few minutes, in 9A, the noise stops. It is as if all the students have synchronized their breaths and emptiness spills into the room.

This is it. Pure Zen. No screaming, no giggling, no hitting, no hats, no soda, nothing but silence. *Oh God.* A girl needs her silence the way she needs coffee in the morning. Normally, that is. But now, I confess. I have gotten used to the din. Inside it I can just stand there, it is camouflage. Nothing is required of me but to make a ceremonial wave upon occasion. And now Erica Reynolds, a good student, a reader of books, a girl who has never been anything but sweet to me, is actually asking a question. A traditional *Shakespearean I-want-to-know question.*

You think I know the answer?

You think I have even recently reread *Romeo and Juliet?*

Did I for one moment think that anybody would do something as impossibly old-fashioned as raise her hand?

What did the Zen master do when he found himself shipwrecked on an island, surrounded by wild beasts?

*Acolytes, he improvised.*

"Actually, Erica," I begin, "*um.* What he meant to do, what it was like, in those days, what he was reaching for . . ."

Natalie cocks an eyebrow.

*She's on to me.*

*I am found out.*

Gibran has sat there in class, at first pleasant to me, then not so pleasant, reading the *Bhagavad Gita*—he is a Hindu—lips moving, then reading nothing at all. He has refused to do any assignment. Every day, like one of those time-collapsed films of plants growing, he increases in sullenness. He sits and plays on the computers in the back of the room. Ask *him* to remove his do-rag? Are you kidding?

And yet. The lights go out, and the first plaintive violins of the *Romeo and Juliet* theme fill the air, and "Shh, I want to hear," says Gibran. The cobbled streets, the towers of an old Italian town, the men in their striped stockings, the women in their velvet gowns: he's there, he's with them, his eyes shine.

He's not familiar with this story, even though *Romeo and Juliet* is still so much part of the cultural air we breathe that it is known by almost everybody else in the room, native and immigrant alike. But somehow it's gone five miles below or above Gibran's radar. Who knows why?

Not that I'm much help. I have explained nothing. I have forgotten how. "What's happening?" he whispers, and someone tells him. And then the dance begins: the stately music, the beautiful lovers-to-be heading toward each other in slow march, hands half raised. "What are they doing?" whispers Gibran.

"It's what they used to do back then," I say. "It's called a pavane."

"Oh." He sighs. "It's beautiful."

I am staring at Gibran. That is what the dark gives me the liberty to do. See him on the street, and he wears the hard protective swagger that makes adults afraid of unknown teenage boys: the power bubbling in them, the daring and physical strength. And here he is, swooning: like some girl at a love story. More like a girl than these girls, frankly.

*Oh, me.*

*Darkling I listen.*

The noise swells, the computers go on, the card games are played. "Check," mumbles Natalie. Tim'n'Bob punch, Elena walks around the room, waggling her butt, and Gibran is sinking: sinking into those palaces, the duels, the lovers parted, the final kiss. Juliet drives in the dagger and falls, and Gibran sighs again, as the lights come on. "It is so sad. It is just so *sad*." His eyes are wet, and I think if he were alone, he might weep.

What can I do with this information, that I've got a romantic on my hands?

Not much. Just let it be a lesson to me: never assume. *Never* assume.

A while later, I will give them an assignment. It is one of my more successful assignments. It carves out one of those pockets of peace that will occur throughout the spring when I least expect it.

A truce, let's say. I ask them to rewrite the balcony scene in modern language, and about a third give it a try. Rosalie invents a coarse rambunctious Juliet, eating peanut butter and jelly on the fire escape, and Adam Patel outswashbuckles Romeo with some pseudo Shakespearean language of his own, and even Maurice stops sleeping and throws some *thees* and *thous* onto a piece of paper.

Gibran wants to give it a try.

He's telling me all the poetic, romantic, over-the-top things his Romeo will say.

"Okay," I say. "Terrific. Write it."

He takes up his pen. He holds it over the page. He puts it down. He can't write it.

"Sometimes it's hard to get started," I say. "Tell me the first line. I'll write it for you."

So he does, and I write it down, and I hand the pen back to him. "Now you."

He puts down an *I*, he writes an *am*. He can go no further.

I am staring at his primitive handwriting. Evidence, I think, of something. This is a boy who wants to. But this is a boy who *can't*.

This is right before the pushpin. After the pushpin, he disappears from class for a while. God knows what is being said to him. Talking about conflict resolution and self-esteem and how the brain, so the theory goes, and maybe it's true, constructs a grid where a tower is what it needs to build. Or maybe they tell him nothing. The school is going charter, there's paperwork to do and bureaucrats to impress. Maybe, at a time like this, a mad pushpinner is someone you just want out of your hair.

Let's face it. There's no way I have the quiet or the patience or the energy to cure a teenage boy of what ails him. Not that I would even know where to begin. And it's kind of a relief, to have one less problem around.

Then one day he reappears. He says nothing about where he's

been, and I ask him nothing. I say hi and he says hi, and then he's gone again.

They have transferred him to another New Visions school, another *small is beautiful every child is a learner* kind of place, where they will figure out, no doubt, what to do with him.

# ANECDOTAL RECORD

Please complete this form whenever there is a need to document student misbehavior and send it to the office for filing. Make extra copies as needed.

Name of student: *Kimberly Franco, Rosalie Smith*

Class: *9A*

Teacher: *Elizabeth Gold*

Date and time of incident: *2ND PERIOD, MAY 4th*

Please describe the problem: *Kimberly and Rosalie were playing their Walkmans so loud I could hear them from the other side of the room. When I asked them to remove the Walkmans, Kimberly said, and I quote: "Fuck you, no." Rosalie thought this was very amusing.*

Please describe the actions you took to address the problem:

*Practiced Zen detachment.*

Every child has a voice. That's what Leon likes to say. Sometimes, as I walk through the halls, head pounding, it seems every child has two voices, *four* voices. Burbling up in the classrooms. By the lockers. In the gym, especially the gym. The stairwells. In the principal's office. Outside the school, where Vincent stands, sophisticated in army jacket and blue eye shadow, smoking a cigarette.

There's the *I know the answer* voice. The *I don't care* voice. The *Fuck you* voice. The *Listen, could you help me?* voice. The *Could I trust you, could I tell you a secret?* voice. The *Please don't call my parents* voice. The *Fuck you, I don't care, call my parents* voice.

The *I'm going to beat the fucking shit out of you* voice.

The *Watch me lie to the principal* voice.

Every child has a voice.

But of course it's not true. It's no more true here than anywhere. Some students choose—or are chosen by—silence. They sit at their desks, as some tempest plays itself out, quietly drawing monsters or unicorns, or reading mysteries or wrestling magazines under the table. Or they do nothing. They sit and they sit, and there is not even a window to look out of. Where they retreat I do not know. Or if there is a voice inside them, whispering, *Wait, this will pass, wait, soon you'll be eighteen, and then twenty-one, and then . . . and then . . .*

I hope they are listening to a voice like that.

I suspect a lot of them are not.

No, not every child has a voice.

But Cindy Fernandez has twelve of them.


They are marvelous, the voices of Cindy Fernandez. They rise and fall, they tremble with ardor and outrage, there is one soft as a baby's. She reminds me of my Communist labor organizer grandmother, long dead now, dead even when I knew her—the cause dead, done in by history, and only her voice, her gorgeous orator's voice, trembling not with the power of the events that were coming, that they, the workers of the world, would make come, but with the events that had passed. Yes, I see in Cindy that kind of power. That raw, that unfeminine, that . . . *eloquent*. The only difference is, my grandmother spoke up for justice, for the new world coming. And Cindy Fernandez, well. She speaks for Cindy Fernandez.

She sits in the back of 9B, a big fat girl crammed into the tiny teen fashions of the day. A mass of nymphet ringlets tumble down her back, but with her plucked brows and matronly bosom, she is nothing like Lolita. She looks years older than the skinny little boys of ninth grade, some of them still staging duels to the death with plastic dinosaurs they smuggle into school. And of course, she *is* older. She is seventeen years old, a seventeen-year-old ninth-grader. Not a stupid girl. Actually, rather a smart one. Yet her peers are almost graduating, and here she sits. And sits and sits and sits. Failing again. Extravagantly failing. Failing with verve and bravado. A mystery to me, because let's face it: ninth grade isn't that interesting the first time around. By the third it must be deadly. So why not try to leave? Tenth grade makes a bit of a change.

Cindy Fernandez. Maria Callas without the soprano. Emma Goldman without the politics. Mae West without the one-liners. A diva without a stage.

Until one day she finds it.

Three weeks into March, I have to give grades.

How can *I* give grades? Even as a kid I didn't care about grades. There was a little bit of the Adam Patel in me. It was *meaning* I cared about, even if I wasn't sure what meaning meant. I was the kind of kid who didn't cheat because to cheat would be to admit that one strove not for enlightenment but for arbitrary approval, and a pat on the head.

Okay, I was a dope. Too high-minded to live. And as is often the case with us high-minded ones, we get ourselves into scrapes that the more sordidly practical avoid.

But still. How can I give grades? I've been here a total of three weeks, which is not very long, but long enough, one would think, to do *something,* but for the life of me, what have we learned except that Britney Spears may—or may not—have acquired breast implants?

*She did.*

*She didn't.*

*She did.*

*She didn't!*

*Oh come on! Nobody grows three sizes overnight!*

*She's just getting fat, that's all!*

*What do you think, Elizabeth?*

*What do I think?*

Grades.

So, okay, I have to give them, but even Leon has realized the absurdity of the situation: one marking period, three teachers, one, at least, with a nervous breakdown. How can I accurately dole out grades?

"Just give the ones who are doing the work an S," he says. "Give the ones who are not, a U. Leave room for comments, then you're done. Can't do much more."

All right, this I can do. *Peter Garcia, S. Sarah Patel, S. Erica Reynolds, S. Alfonso, the brilliant, eccentric Alfonso . . . well, what do you expect?*

U.

It unnerves me, writing down the grades. I try, a little bit, to give people points not simply for *doing* it, but for attempting to think, but it's not easy. The push to give reward merely for showing up is strong. If I don't, I've got an 80 percent failure rate on my hands, maybe more. But what do I do with those crumpled scraps handed to me? What are they evidence of? Learning disabilities? If they are—and how do I really know?—how am I supposed to evaluate them? And if not learning disabilities, what's the problem? Emotional disabilities? Grand Ennui? Or is it too much self-esteem, the idea that any old thing you do is wonderful, because so are you?

Are they simply missing Sharon, or April? The instability of the universe getting them down? That's Leon's theory.

*Man*, I don't know.

Go through the motions, I think. They don't care. Haven't I heard Alan and David and Randolph and Sammy cry out when I finally resorted to the dullest teacher trick in the book, the threat of failure, haven't I heard them say, *I don't care, I'll just go to summer school?*

Didn't seem like much of a solution to me, who wants to be in school in the middle of July? I don't, and I would get paid for it. But I guess if a kid is poor, if there is no camp to go to and he's too young to get a job, or if he simply suffers from lack of imagination, summer school relieves the mind from trying to figure out what happens next, it provides institutional comfort and torpor.

*Robert, S. Ahmed, S. Ken, S. Silvia, U. Adam, S. David, Randolph, Sammy, Ricardo, Jose, Lucille, Cindy, U, U, U, U, U, U, U.*

Do they really expect anything different?


In a few days, it will be Parent Teacher Night—a night I dread. The grades will be handed out then. But surprisingly, one morning, the kind of quiet that falls upon a classroom right before the grades are given out, a kind of exhausted anticipation, suddenly overcomes 9B.

"You know," announces Cindy, "no one in the ninth grade is going to get credit for English class."

She announces it so authoritatively that immediately almost everyone accepts it as true. Hell, *I* accept it as true.

And that means summer school, she says. *Everyone* is going to summer school.

At that second, she's done it. She's shaken the champagne

bottle. She's worried out the cork, and now those voices the students have are spraying round the room. Everything they have hated about the School of the New Millennium, everything that, with all their complaints, they kept inside, it's out now. All the teachers coming and going, the chaos of things beginning, the promises made and not delivered, it's all out now, and there's so much fury in the classroom, that teachers start getting accused of crimes that are hardly crimes—Vivian, for instance, who had the temerity to get . . . pregnant, yes, pregnant, how dare she, didn't she know she was going to need three months of emergency bed rest, shouldn't the school have made plans? Shouldn't they have known? Why should the students suffer for all the fumblings of adults, why should *they* all have to go to summer school?

Never have I seen the students so galvanized, candy and Walkmans and Britney Spears forgotten.

"We need to talk to the other classes," says Cindy. *"I'll* talk to them. We've got to demand our rights. We'll make sure no one goes to summer school! No one!"

"Uh, Cindy," I start to say, "some people will go to summer school, no matter what . . ."

But Cindy pays no attention. "After all," she announces, "I'm seventeen, older than any of you, I've been here longer than any of you, I *know* what this place is like."

And now I'm thinking how ridiculous it is, that she should be seventeen and here. Raging against summer school when she shouldn't even be going to summer school at all. This girl has a brain, and no fat girl shyness, she is more than willing to shine. So why has she squandered her power?

I don't know. But I know that people do. I know that some-times the only power you think you've got is the power to throw it away.

*I don't care, I don't care, I don't care.*

So, the students are busy organizing, I don't know exactly what they're doing, but now I am the one who doesn't care. Let them organize. Get their complaints and confusions out of their systems. Let us begin again with mutual acceptance, and good will. Meanwhile, I'm puzzling over the riddle of Cindy Fernan-dez. All those years of failure.

Suddenly I make a decision: *I will save her.*

She is in trouble, and I will rescue her, and I think I know how.

You see, she and I have something in common. Not only a cer-tain self-destructive streak, a talent for resentment, but something else: Cindy is a poet. She belongs to the spoken-word-here-are-my-feelings-they've-never-been-felt-before teenage school of po-etry. Of course I have heard it before, but it doesn't matter. She's got some talent, and some feeling, she's got *something,* does Cindy Fernandez.

What would happen if I recognized that something?

Now I'm the one who's high on power: I will show her the world, I will remake her, I will save Cindy Fernandez.

Independent study, I think. She's old enough to be removed from the classroom, and surely it must be humiliating to be sitting here, the oldest student in the room. So we'll study poetry to-gether. We'll read Dickinson, and Neruda, and Ahkmatova. Clas-sics. Why not? She's got the brain for it, I know it. She'll write her own poems, of course she will, and attend a poetry reading, and give a poetry reading—a dramatic girl like her would blow any audience away—and together, on my own time, we will fight for Cindy Fernandez. I will give her the recognition I craved, but never got for myself.

That'll give her something more challenging than summer school to think about.

And then it is the end of class, and the students rise to their feet, and as Cindy Fernandez is leaving the room, I stop her, and tell her my plan.

"What do you think?" I say. "You could really do it. It would be a challenge, but you could really do it. You would like it. You could really *learn* something, you know? You really could."

Are there tears in her eyes? And is she crying because of my offer, or because of the exhaustion of being Cindy Fernandez?

"Okay," she says. Acting like she's doing *me* a favor.

But I've been seventeen. I know how difficult gratitude can be.

I massage the School of the New Millennium knot in the back of my neck. "Good. We'll talk about it tomorrow."

She smiles weakly and leaves the room.

But I am not alone. Peter Garcia is standing in a corner, watching me.

He has not participated in any of the uproar, though Peter Garcia does have a voice—two voices as a matter of fact. His *I love skateboarding* voice and the other voice he uses to get around his world and to define it. They are both voices I like, though the first I hear only while eavesdropping—it is the voice reserved for the other boys who love skateboarding, too. The second is the one he uses with me. That voice is honest and direct and clear. Peter

Garcia never wheedles or rails. He doesn't know how. He doesn't want to. What he does is tell it like he sees it, and he sees a lot, does Peter Garcia.

"Hey," I say. "What's up?"

"I wrote something for you," he says. "I just want you to read it."

*Some people are hypocrites,* he has written. *They demand their rights, but they never want anybody else to have any.*

I feel hot, weak, embarrassed. I know who he's talking about. Have I made a miscalculation?

"Oh, Peter," I say. "Maybe if she speaks she'll get it out of her system."

He shakes his head and sighs.

Oh, the stupidity of adults. The well-meaningness of their mistakes. What else can Peter Garcia do but practice patient forbearance?

For he knows a lot. I don't know how he picked it up or if it's just an innate something in him, but he knows. And in a little while, if I'm smart enough and pay enough attention, I might know a little bit, too.

Adam Patel is happy.

As a pig in mud, as a cow in clover, as a gold digger on the arm of a very old tycoon.

Cindy has just come in to class 9A and announced the emergency school meeting—or Town Meeting, as it's called in the lingo of the New Millennium—and Adam has visions. Adam, poring over his little stash of 1960s newspapers, has been waiting for this most of his life.

Reform. Revolution.

He's standing there, surveying his class, and for him, a complaint or two about grades is *nothing*. It's the beginning. History is cyclical. The Free Speech movement started small. But it started, that's the thing.

"We're all going to summer school. We're all going, unless we *do* something," Cindy says, and just as in 9B, these words open up all the discontent and fury inside the kids, and all of them, from the snoozers and solitaire players to the one idealist, are in an uproar: Natalie and I do nothing but stand back and watch. Off they go, that litany of complaints, back, back, through ninth grade, then eighth, and seventh, all the plagues that swept the school long before I arrived, and I remember now what it once felt like, that pure anger at how the world goes wrong.

Then Vincent, class clown, prince of the elaborate, time-wasting gesture, opens up the cabinets in the back of the room.

"*OH MY GOD!*" he gasps. "Do you *see?*"

Piled in the cabinet are dozens of portfolios. He grabs a few, and other students do, too. They're flipping through them.

"These are the portfolios we did for Sharon," Vincent explains to me. "She was supposed to grade them. Do you see any grades? Do you see any?"

"Think of the work!" Vincent continues, brandishing one of the folders. "Think of the hours and hours of hard labor! The hours I *would* have labored if I *had* done it! I mean, I did nothing. But what if I had done something? It would have been the same as if I had done *nothing*. I mean, I *deserve* nothing, I *know* that, but what if I *deserved* something? It's not fair! It's not fair!"

Adam Patel is miserable.

He has come in to 9C, accompanied by Maurice, who looks re-markably unstoned for once, hoping to inspire the class to ask questions and work together for the betterment of all.

"I don't care!" Sammy Morales shouts. "I don't care! I'm going to summer school anyway!"

Randolph gives him an affectionate punch.

Jose, having lifted his head to see what's up, adjusts his sweater and lies once more across the table.

"You see what we're up against?" I say to Adam, with probably too much triumph in my voice.

"Oh man," he groans, burying his face in his hands, "Oh man, oh man, oh man."

Somewhere between Adam's joy in 9A and despair in 9C I get this idea. It comes to me on little cat feet, or rosy-fingered, like the dawn. *I've got a job offer, right? A really good job offer. And I can't be fired, right? And I need books. Real books.* Not books with charts and arrows in them and a paragraph or two on *the writing process* but old-fashioned, ordinary books, books that can be taken home and read.

*Why don't I ask?*

Ask? Asking is for sissies. Better: demand. Justice is, after all, on my side.

What would a general do? Not beg. I know that. Demand, for the betterment of all.

I sit right down and write Leon a letter. It feels good. I'm not doing much of my own writing right now, I'm just too tired, even when I get enough sleep. But this letter reminds me: I am a writer. I write.

I'm eloquent, too, if I say so myself. It's because I know I can say anything. So why *not* say anything?

So this is what power feels like.

You know? It's very pleasant.

And now the day of the Town Meeting arrives. We file into the auditorium, which is just a big room filled with folding chairs, and if I have any hope that I will simply witness what I've helped put into motion, the hope is dashed by the arrangement of those chairs. The students are to sit in one group, and we, the teachers of the ninth grade, are to sit in a row facing them, Cultural Revolution style.

Why do I feel sick to my stomach?

I sit down next to Vivian. She is a round-faced woman with a head of neat, rather dashing dreads, and an angelic smile that is probably excellent to hide behind.

*"Hey,"* I whisper.

She smiles the smile. I would like to take her hand.

"Okay, okay, to order," says Leon. "This is a very good thing we're doing. This is democracy in action. Talking about our problems and solving them together. This is how we learn to become leaders. As a family. Soon I'll open the floor."

At first, it's so civilized and sensible I start to relax. Students like Erica and Adam start talking about teachers coming and going, and about their credits, and what's going to happen next, and what they'd like to have happen next, and *democracy*, I think, this is okay, this is even interesting. What a genius I am for having listened to Cindy. Just think how those questions and resentments would have bubbled under the surface if I hadn't.

Vincent stands up and asks about the folders.

Turns out the folders were from last semester. They had already been marked, and their grades given to the students in the fall.

I find myself, kidlike, rolling my eyes. Surely they must have recognized those folders. All that rage, and for what?

Then Vincent starts talking about Vivian. For three months, he says, his voice trembling, for three months, they had substitute science teachers, teachers who didn't know anything, while *she* lay around in bed. Didn't they know how disruptive this was going to be? Why didn't they make plans?

Poor old Vincent. So savvy. So cool. So . . .

*fifteen.* It's the pregnancy that bugs him, the scary thought of teacher sex and teacher burgeoning; the thought that we live, in the burrow of our dark adult lives we live, and even take off our clothes.

"You bitch," I mumble to Vivian. "How could you do that to Vincent, getting pregnant like that, didn't you have any regard for his feelings?"

We giggle, and then Nestor stands.

Nestor, possessor of class 9A's strongest ass.

"Our problem," he says, "is that we're not bonding with the new English teacher."

*Oh. So it's like that.*

Funny what a good tool Sensitivity Language is. What a brutal tool. You can't argue with it, you can't say that *feelings* are not important, when we know, of course, that they are the only thing that count.

Not that you should say, out loud, anyway, that you hate the English teacher.

Say, you can't *bond* with her. Then we can discuss your tender feelings, and the inability of the English teacher to take them seriously. Her fault, you know. What a monster she is.

Suddenly I notice that the only people in this room who do *not* have a voice are the teachers. We are supposed to sit there and listen. But I've heard enough, enough.

I'm almost on my feet.

*Bonding, Nestor?* I want to shout. *Isn't it bondage you mean? Admit it! Don't you want to tie me up and stomp my face?*

"We've run out of time," Tom announces. "Let's go back to class."

God bless Tom.

Parent Teacher Night is a nightmare.

I clean my room from top to bottom, buy flowers and put them on my desk, I dress well, and sit there with my hands folded, waiting.

Then they come: The ones who blame me for their children's failure, though their children have failed before. The ones whose children have never failed before, the parents sitting there baffled, while the chastened kids sob in the corner, saying piteously, *"I'll be good, I'll be good, next semester, I'll be good."* The parents waving the *U* in my face, demanding, *"I want to see you teach!"*

Hey, me, too.

Mrs. Garcia weeps. She's divorced, harried, speaks with a thick accent.

"Oh, he doesn't blame you. He *likes* you. But he comes home and he says, *Mami. El ruido. Me duele la cabeza.*"

Oh God. My class makes Peter Garcia's head hurt.

"I'm sorry," I say. "I'm sorry, I'm sorry, I'm sorry."

"Not your fault," she says.

But whose fault is it?

At the end of the next day, I'm sitting in my classroom, slumped over my desk, when Naomi walks in. She is one of the mothers who works in the office, and like a lot of the parents involved with the running and philosophy of the school, well meaning, progressive, and white.

"How's it going?" she says.

I laugh.

"I'm sorry you're having a hard time," she says, looking at me sympathetically. "If you were like Nkruma, it would be different. The kids listen to him. He's got a lot of charisma."

She smiles warmly. "But you're like me. We've got no charisma."

*Well well well.*

Naomi has decided to share.

The month is almost over. It is hard to believe: that it has only been a month, and that it is over. To celebrate, a little square of spring shows up in our small window. And I find myself in 9C, the last class of the day, and suddenly my favorite one.

How could 9C be my favorite class? More to the point: how could it be the only class I am not afraid of?

Yet it does make sense. For one thing, I have requested that the most disruptive students—Randolph and Sammy—be removed for a little while, to do an assignment I have designed as discipline, and I guess, punishment, before they are allowed to return.

Leon, knowing how close I am to quitting, has agreed.

I know it's a stopgap, and they'll be back, they'll be back even though there is no way they could do the difficult assignment I have invented for them. But for now, there is peace. It is astonishing what a difference the absence of two students has made.

Even Jose takes the sweater off his head.

I suppose it is undemocratic to just wish these guys would go away, but I am not the only one wishing it. In the week they are gone, the students who formerly did nothing find themselves working, participating, being *nice*.

How pleasant it is to discover I am not a child hater.

9C.

I wouldn't say a lot of their skills are great. This is still the depository of the students with difficulties—language, emotional, learning—difficulties so huge some of them can barely write their names. This is the class of boys who have given up. Faced with this range, and with little in the way of assistance or material, I don't know what to do with them.

The strange thing is, every once in a while I bring in something that catches their fancy. I just can't predict what it will be, and it doesn't seem to make a difference the next day. A good day never seems to buy you another good day.

Still. Suddenly I find 9C . . . relaxing.

Maybe it's true that more than half of them are going to go to summer school. But they don't blame me for it. No. 9C decided long before I walked in the door that summer school is where they were going. It is their destiny. They can see no other. They have failed before. They will fail again. What difference does a *U* make in a lifetime of *Fs?*

If you recognize your fate walking down the empty road, embrace it. Give it a bear hug.

Is this not Zen? Can I not learn from them? Is not the American fear of failure, of things going awry and then other things going awry, the terror of that pinball machine exploding, a spiritual mistake?

In the beginning, after all, despite the propaganda, there was not a Word, carefully pronounced in a quiet room after much work with the speech teacher, but a boiling up of gas. It wasn't precision that made the universe, it was chaos, a tumult in the dark. So say then that 9C has plunged me back into our primal creative moment, when there were no surprise quizzes or charts to fill out and every day was a multiple choice exam and the answer was always D: *None of the Above.*

We are tired, 9C.

We have tired ourselves out, the lot of us.


In the still of this particular afternoon, this sleepy, woozy, Friday aftermath of revolution, Alan lifts his head from his assignment, which, to his and my surprise, he is doing, with competence, and looks through the windows that face the hall.

"Why is there a fireman out there?"

And so there is. In full regalia: black rubber hat, black coat, and is he holding an axe?

*Ohboyohboyohboyohboy.* "There's a fire!" cries 9C, happily. "A fire! A fire! We're going to burn up! We're going to burn *alive!*"

I am gazing and gazing through the glass at this stranger, this . . . *fireman.*

*Oh my God.*

I have lasted a month, and now they have sent me . . .

*a fireman.*

He is striding slowly down the hall in silence, and even from this distance, waves of his firemanliness waft into the room like smoke.

What is it about firemen?

I admit it, it's corny, but I just love them.

What is it about firemen, girls?

As metaphors, they're flawed. I mean, think of miners. The way they tunnel into the earth, down through the muck and the rock, pulling gold from the deepest, most unlikely places. When it's a lover you're dreaming of, wouldn't a miner be the man you want, a man who could do that sort of thing, and not once, but day after day and *all* day? Hot *damn*. Or scuba divers, say, there's an image to get you going. Those vulnerable bodies resting for a moment on the rim of the boat and then allowing themselves to tumble into the sea, that mother of us all, that ebb and float and gravity, the hiding place for monsters and schools of fish like handfuls of jewels let loose, now there's a lover for you, a man whose world is water, *salt* water, its sting like tears or sweat, isn't that the kind of lover we want, a man with that much enthusiasm for surrender?

How could a fireman compete with that much extravagance?

Oh, but he does, he does.

"Let me find out what's going on," I announce to the class.

I walk into the hall. I love the hall, especially when there are no students in it. In the middle of a typical noisefest, I have found myself looking out into the silence and emptiness of the hall with longing. So peaceful. So Zen.

And it's still Zen. It's just Zen with Fireman.

His back is to me. He's walking away.

"Excuse me," I say.


I was rescued once.

A few summers ago, the subway train I was riding on got stuck in a tunnel. An incomprehensible announcement crackled over the PA system, and the lights went off, and the air-conditioning, and so we sat, in the dark, in the heat, for hours, and then we were rescued.

I suppose you could say it started then, Dr. Freud. Not with the primal symbolism of axe and hose but there: after hours of taking deep breaths, waiting for something to happen, when the doors were pried open. And perched on a ladder, floating in that doorway like a rubberized angel, was a fireman.

"You okay in there?"

The words of course, you're always waiting for.

"Sure," we said. "Fine, we're fine."

To say anything else would have been *outre*. Does one complain to an angel? Wrestle with, maybe. But whine?

*Oh please.*

"I've come to get you out," he said.

He took us one by one down the ladder. And I don't know how it was for anyone else, but in my case, he was right below, talking the whole time, in a soft calm voice.

"I'm right below you," he said. "Don't worry. Don't be scared. Almost there. Are you all right?"

"I'm fine," I said. "Fine, fine, fine . . ."

Then I, with a crowd of passengers, was standing at the bottom of the black tunnel.

The New York subway tunnel. The one usually glimpsed from the safety of the platform.

I've seen rats skittering through this tunnel. Big rats. Heavyweight rats. Sumo rats. And yet, strangely, very speedy rats. Rats unafraid of a big crowd.

"*Ohhh*," we breathed. "Don't look down."

Then came the voices. Not one, but a chorus of them.

*Are you all right? Are you all right?*

There they were. Standing against the walls of the tunnel as far as I could see. Firemen. Expressing their concern. And meaning it. Every word, I'm *positive*.

*Follow the light,* they said, *you're almost there, the end of the tunnel.*

Yes I know. A cliché. But there was a light. And an end. And a tunnel.

Dutifully we started marching. It's what they wanted us to do, and you want to make men like this happy.

Still. Why didn't I say it?

*Take me.*

*Take me, take me. Here, by the wheels of the train, right here, in the hollow of the third rail, in the rubble, in the trash, rats? What rats? Take me. You can keep your raincoat on. In fact, I prefer it. Just . . . just . . .*

*take me.*

Then I will be all right.


"What's going on here?" I say.

"Oh, it's just a routine. Fire inspection."

"Find anything?" I say.

"Not a thing."

"Too bad."

I am gazing at him. What can I say? Friday afternoon, and here he is . . .

My fireman is blond.

I usually don't go for blonds, but firemen are different. Firemen are blond so their hair will be light in a disaster. So when the smoke is billowing there is still something that does not belong to the dark.

I smile at him. He smiles back.

My fireman is no kid: lines radiate from his blue eyes, lines I would love to trace with a finger, they are so sexy and knowing. As for his coat, his black rubber coat with the buckles, those brass buckles I long to slide open with a satisfying snap . . . *oh*. My fireman. With his manly aura, his aura of . . . fireman.

As I am standing there, for I don't know how long, the din in room 313 begins.

A soft rumble at first, like a train heard from far away, the message sent along the rails and then a *quit* and a *stop* and a *fuck you*, the resound of what can only be two desks or three transformed into bumper cars.

My fireman gives me a very adult, companionable smirk.

"Save me," I whisper. *"Save me."*

"All right," he says. "I'll save you."

Is this not evidence, good ladies and gentlemen of the jury, of my sense of responsibility and duty to these kids, these leaders I am leading toward tomorrow, that I sacrifice myself, I think of my love for these children, I do not budge, I stay exactly where I am?

TO ALL 9TH GRADE PARENTS:

THERE IS GOING TO BE A VERY
IMPORTANT MEETING
AT THE SCHOOL OF THE NEW MILENIUM
WEDNESDAY, MARCH 29, 2000 5:00 P.M.
AGENDA: ENGLISH CLASS
YOU MUST ATTEND!!!
WE WILL NOT ACCEPT FAILING
GRADES FOR OUR CHILDREN!!!!!

PARA TODO LOS PADRES DEL NOVENO GRADO.
VAMOS A TENER UNA REUNIÓN MUY
IMPORTANTE EN LA ESCUELA
NEW MILLENNIUM
MIÉRCOLES, MARZO 29, 2000, 5:00 P.M.
AGENDA: LA CLASE DE INGLES
USTEDES, SIENDO LOS PADRES,
TENEMOS QUE LUCHAR POR EL BIEN
DE NUESTRO HIJOS/AS.
NO VAMOS ACEPTAR ESTE FRACASO
PARA NUESTRO NIÑOS/AS

april
**school property**

I do not go.

That flyer, the one where they spelled *Millennium* wrong? The one with the ringing battle cry, *We Will Not Accept Failing Grades For Our Children?* I'm given a copy. I'm given *several* copies.

But I do not go. So I can't tell you who is there. I can't describe the stirring speeches, or the moment when Cindy Fernandez comes to the floor and describes how all semester she did nothing, and then the new English teacher, in the tradition of the old English teachers, had the nerve to give her an unsatisfactory grade.

Ah, yes.

Once we fought for justice, for the rights of the working man, for the freedom to vote and live and work where we want, for the end of the War in Vietnam. But that is just so old hat. We've got *real* issues to discuss.

Grades.

Democracy in action. Too bad I have to miss it. My calendar, it turns out, is full. I spend the night in question lying in bed, drinking Scotch and rereading old detective stories.

No doubt it is thrilling, the young people trembling with power, and Leon sitting there, listening carefully, for every child has a voice, and every parent, too. But I have a serious dental flossing session lined up, and I've been putting it off for weeks. I can't reschedule.

Besides, nobody asks me.

"You are in big trouble," Cindy Fernandez says, barreling into the room, "Big Trouble. There was a meeting last night, and where were you?"

This is the moment I should say, *What meeting?* or, *Sorry, family emergency,* or, *Too bad, I was busy speaking last night at the World Conference for Soda and Hats.*

"Nobody asked me," I say.

"Oh, we asked you," says Lucille.

Why have I never noticed how *big* she is? How truly muscular, shoulders like . . .

"It was a very interesting meeting," Cindy announces, "very very interesting. We talked about . . . *you.*"

Beautiful. A paranoid's dream come true.

I have handed out a story, "The Lottery," as a matter of fact, and what could be more appropriate? Some of the students, more inured to chaos than I seem to be able to get, are trying to read it. My admiration for them, their stubborn persistence in grasping at the good, is increasing daily. But after a while, even they have to stop.

"Oh yes. We talked about you. About how horrible you are. And you were supposed to be there. We needed to talk to you. Why weren't you there?" says Cindy.

She shakes her head. "I just don't get it," says Cindy. "How could someone as stupid as you *ever* be a teacher?"

There goes her independent study. I start working on my own: how to keep cool in one easy lesson. My emergency juices are pumping overtime, and a little voice, my Inner Yogi, is saying in my head, *Deep breaths, deep breaths, the light touch of the fingers on the eyes, ears, nose, and lips shuts off the disturbance of the external world. . . .*

"Look at her," Lucille says. "She can't handle us. She can't handle *anybody*. She's pathetic. She thinks this is bad? She doesn't know what's bad. We'll show her bad. Throw her in Newtown! Throw her in Bryant! See how she'll survive. She *won't*. And *she* taught college? Oh, come on! I don't believe it! If she can't handle us, how could she have handled college? I'd like to see *her* in college!"

"No shit," says Marcy enthusiastically.

*I'd like to see you in college. Harvard is salivating. They need someone to rearrange their broom closets.*

"Oh," says Cindy, "we're going to tear this school *down*." She nods, sagely. "I'm going to call the *New York Times*. I know people there. They'll be very interested in what's going on here."

*Yes. I can see it now. Banner headlines: Seventeen-Year-Old Ninth-Grader, Does Nothing and Fails Class, Unhappy With Bad Grades.*

"We're going to get you fired, Elizabeth. We're going to get you *all* fired," Cindy continues. "Once people find out what's been going on here, you think this school is going to last? No way! Do you think they care about us? They *don't*. They just care about their jobs. And now they're scared. They're all going to get fired and they're *scared*."

It's true. I am scared. I'm scared that I'm *not* going to lose my job. That no matter what happens, my job is going to stick to me, like that fairy tale when the fisherman's wife wishes that a sausage would get stuck on her husband's nose and then no one can get it off.

My job is that sausage.

I tried to help her, I think, feebly, but now I get it, now I understand what Peter Garcia was trying to tell me.

Cindy Fernandez wasn't grateful when I offered to help her. She was put on the spot. It meant she would have to *do* something. It meant that she would one day graduate from ninth grade, and she doesn't want to graduate. She's afraid of tenth grade. Afraid of the world. She wants this, only the misery of this. She wants her anger. She wants the glory of the stage, the drama of her own degradation. *Listen, I should know what I'm talking about. I'm the oldest person in this room. I'm an eighty-five-year-old ninth-grader. Ninth grade? Ask me anything. I'm an expert.*

She wants the deliciousness of her own grievance.

I don't say a word. What is there to say? I can't silence them. And I can't state the obvious, either, that these girls are going nowhere, when I am so obviously nowhere myself.

"This class is so long," sighs Cindy melodramatically. "I can't stand it, it's so boring, it's so long, when is it ever going to be over?"

"I wish all the classes were short," says Lucille. "If only they were shorter."

"But then our class with Nkruma would be short," says Cindy. "And every minute in his class, it's wonderful, we learn so *much*, I wouldn't want it shorter by a minute, that would be terrible, so I guess we'll have to have this stupid boring class with stupid Elizabeth so we can have our class with Nkruma."

I've backed myself as deep into my corner as I can, and as for my metal desk, I have never been so grateful for a piece of furniture in my life. And somehow I find myself looking up. Looking toward—who else—Peter Garcia.

He is gazing at me. What a look—what a grown up, sympathetic look.

*Peter Garcia.*

"Ignore her," he says. "Everybody does."

*Peter Garcia, Peter Garcia.*

It is wrong, wrong, morally wrong to envy the Tamale Lady. Look at her, how she stands at the foot of the number-seven stairs, day after day, in all weathers: rain, wind, noisome heat. She's there, the Tamale Lady. She doesn't get a day off. She doesn't have health insurance. She doesn't have a pension. She doesn't even have a regular paycheck. She earns her pennies husk by husk and lump of corn meal by lump of corn meal. Let that be a metaphor for you, the hardness and heartbreak of human labor. On the covers of the magazines, impossibly cute millionaires recline in their ski hideaways, confessing that while they work twenty hours a day, it is *family, their beautiful family, that really matters. But of course, they love their work, too!* Turn your face from that magazine, those attractive people in attractive clothes bending over a computer screen. That is not work. That is a ghost cast upon some glass. This is work, the ancient work, labor that bends backs and gnarls hands in the alleyways of Alexandria, under the trees in Tashkent, in the sunbaked square—that white sun, the sun that hacks great lines in the face—of Timbuktu. This is work that pulls her out of bed at dawn, that splashes cold water on the cheeks and gets the coffee pumping in the dark, all in the dark: the water bubbling in battered pots, the stir of corn meal, cracked fingers filling the husks and tying up each package tight. This is work that has robbed her of whatever beauty she might have owned for a while: No time or money for dentists, face buffed by the weather so she is of any or no imaginable age, her body encased in old sweaters and a lumpy tweed coat like a badly wrapped package of butcher's meat.

And of course, her voice grown hoarse with crying: *Tamales. Tamales. Tamales.*

Labor is a curse.

So forgive me, forgive me. Because I *do* envy the Tamale Lady.

I envy her freedom in the air, the open air, standing out there on the street while the shops roll up their iron gates and the day stirs itself like a creature waking. It is good to be witness to the beginning of things, even on—or maybe, especially on—a dirty street such as this. I envy her the pleasure of making those tamales, the wet gold taking shape, the smell of the corn meal, the satisfaction of folding each husk: *done.* Who could argue with this, the necessity of tamales? I watch her each morning as I run down the subway station stairs, too culturally shy to buy a tamale for myself. I watch the laborers come up and smile at her politely and I watch her lift the lid of the canister and steam billow up. *Listen to them talk to each other.* I could stand there and do it for hours. *Hola. Buenos días.* What softness. What gentleness. *Por favor.* It lies on my tongue like a coin of warm corn meal. How did my life get so harsh?

*You just have to have a dream. You can do it!* That's what they say at the School of the New Millennium. So this is my dream: to start all over again. To learn Spanish in the cradle and the art of tamale making when I am barely old enough to walk. To leave my country and, in the shade of the girders, to reinvent it for the rest of my life: with the sound of *cumbia*. The smoothness of guava paste. The secret heat—the heat tucked deep inside the skin of lesser heat—of tamales.

*. . . Number-seven train.*

How could I be so tired at eight in the morning?

This is me, Liz, co-conspirator with the dawn. I *like* morning. Me and the larks, we know what's what. Morning is good. Morning is the best. I have irritated more late-night slugabeds than I can count by my talent for waking early, cheerfully, and at once. No need to be pulled into morning; morning is pulling me. That first cup of coffee as I stare out the window at the street unrolling its scrubbed and empty self is my covenant with the day. Our pact that after all, things will turn out all right.

But now. I cannot sleep enough.

And while nothing can quite ruin that first cup of coffee—though it's almost like a memory of a first cup of coffee that I'm drinking—I am *tired*.

The doors open. The doors close.

Number seven train.

At this hour, most travelers are going the other way, from Queens to Manhattan. But in my commute, there's never a problem getting a seat. There's just a drowsy handful of us in this car. It only adds to my feeling that I've managed this neat trick of falling off the planet yet am somehow still walking around on it.

*Oh me.*

How pleasant it is to be sitting here, where not a soul is compelled to tell me how horrible I am. How sweet, how snoozily sweet, is the train's slow rhythm, as it takes the curves as if it can hardly be bothered to take them.

I could fall asleep on this train. It would be easy.

I could give up any pretext of verticality, of purpose and places to go. I could lay my head down on my knapsack and dream a little dream of Queens Plaza, of Roosevelt Boulevard, of Shea Stadium, all the way out to Flushing, land of Utopia Parkway and Nirvana Boulevard. Then back to Times Square, and out again.

Always going someplace. Never arriving. I could be the Flying Dutchman of this train. My next career path. All motion. No voice. *Yes.*

But somehow, like the census job, it fades. I've got no courage, I guess.

And now we're almost at my stop, and with a sigh, I reach for my knapsack, ready to sling it over my shoulder.

But it's not going.

It sits there on the seat, lumpishly, stubbornly refusing to lift.

I tug this time.

Can a knapsack practice civil disobedience?

Me and objects, we've always had an uneasy truce. Things want to break on me. Wheelchairs hurl themselves at me. And now my knapsack is refusing to move.

I look down and see that the buckle on one of the straps has worked its way into a crack between two seats. A freakish accident, but as Freud said, there are no accidents.

I slide the strap up and down the crack, hoping to work it free, but that buckle shows a remarkable talent for holding on.

Almost there.

Tugging harder, now. I'm beginning to panic as I mull over the alternatives: One, to empty my knapsack of keys, books, note-book, pens, brush, loose change, wallet, tampons, and the ever important wadded-up tissues, and run to school with this stuff in my arms, looking more professional than ever. The other is to just keep riding. Which somehow doesn't sound as tempting as it did when it was pure imagination.

Now we are at my stop. The doors open.

"Hold the doors!" I cry, and then I get one more idea.

"Anybody have scissors? Something sharp? *Anything?*"

A man in overalls reaches into his toolbox and takes out a very large knife.

*Ahhhh,* sighs the car.

As he's walking toward me, holding up that big, beautiful knife of his, I realize there could be a sick little twist to this tale, I could be on the front page of the *Daily News* tomorrow. Never mind. One way or the other, there's an ending to this story.

*Thhwack.*

I am free.

Well. No time for semantics here. I possess freedom of move-ment, anyway.

And with that freedom I am running out of the car, knapsack over my shoulder, trying not to think of the obvious:

Even my knapsack doesn't want to go to school.

As Leon suggested, I am barraging my students with work—puzzles, vocabulary exercises, open-book exams so easy you'd have to be dead to get them wrong:

*Mrs. Maloney takes deep breaths because*
    *a. she is anxious*
    *b. she is nervous*
    *c. she has lungs*
    *d. all of the above*

It is so easy, some of them cry, looking at their 85s, and their hundreds, so easy, and that's the point, to win them over with so many carrots they practically glow in the dark. And then, says Leon, they will find out how good it feels, academic achievement, we will bring those kids along.

"Okay, kids, I'm sending around another quiz," I scream, since the din never stops. "Here it comes."

Cindy Fernandez is ripping up her quiz. Lucille and Marcy join her.

"I didn't get a quiz," Cindy announces. "Elizabeth didn't send a quiz to me. And then, look. She is going to give me a zero. *She* didn't give me a quiz, and then *I* have to pay for it. Is that fair? She fails me for not doing the work, and she doesn't give me the work!"

"Oh, look!" cries Lucille, looking out the window. "There's Leon! Let's tell him!"

Out they run.

I hate to see the way 9B has unzipped and rezipped itself. It gives me a prickly, anxious feeling, a sensation of racial dread. On Cindy Fernandez's side sit the black and Latino students. On Peter Garcia's side sit the Latino, and what do we call them?— Italian-American — Irish-American — Jewish-American — Slavic-American?—Oh, I'm sick of the whole damn thing.

It wasn't always this way. Or at least, not completely. Andrew Santangelo, the big, plump, giggling, rosy-cheeked boy who has, I think, a crush on tiny, skinny, black Marcy, used to sit next to her, reading *Catcher in the Rye* and sometimes giving her little pokes and noogies that you know mean love. Then one day Andrew picked up his book and sat down near Peter Garcia. Which is where he stays. Transformation of room complete.

The weird thing is, the thing that confuses me, it's not the black students who decide their side is black. It is Cindy Fernandez, and I guess, to be just, also the dark Lucille, but mainly it is Cindy Fernandez, who is not black at all, but the palest apricot.

Oh, it is a dark place, a dark American place, Room 313, a place of confusing tribal identification, for Peter Garcia has probably less in common with Tim'n'Bob, trying to brain each other with metal trucks, than with Stephen Thomas, who lets Cindy Fernandez incite him to act like a moron and then watches himself act like a moron, thinking—I can see him thinking—*Damn. What a moron.*

*Mrs. Maloney walks to the door because*
  *a. she wants to open it*
  *b. she can't fly there*
  *c. the door won't walk to her*
  *d. all of the above*

Now I'm sitting here, pretending to watch some of my students ace the latest quiz when what I'm really watching is Cindy, Lucille, and Marcy explain to Leon how awful I am, how unfair and crazy, while he stands there in Listening Mode, arms folded, very serious. Does he believe them? It doesn't matter if he believes them. He just wants them to know he is Listening. When their voice is heard, their self-esteem will spiral up, and when that happens . . .

Look out, world.

*Mrs. Maloney prefers oral sex because*
  *a. aural sex is not so exciting*
  *b. choral sex is just too loud*
  *c. moral sex? There's no such thing*
  *d. none of the above*

No, no, no. I didn't write it. I wasn't even tempted.

Well, maybe tempted. A girl's gotta keep herself amused, you know?

A brief lull in the room. The easiness of the quiz, and the few bonus questions, the ones that actually require thinking, are pulling the students in despite themselves. They are scribbling away, and I don't know if St. Jude, the saint of lost causes, accepts the prayers of unJewish Jews such as myself, but I'm sending one up: *Thanks, big guy.*

This is when Cindy, Lucille, and Marcy run back into the room. Looking flushed, pretty, triumphant.

Until, that is, they see Zuleika and Marie and Charles working, and looking very pleased with themselves, too.

"What do you want to do that for?" Cindy says. "Why do you want to act so white?"

Peter Garcia throws down his pen.

"And what are you?" he says.

You want to be a good teacher? Forget brains. Forget wit. Forget imagination. Forget a good sense of humor. Forget even empathy. These things are nice, and will make you a pleasant companion over dinner, but if you want to succeed at the teaching biz, what you need are a strong index finger and a steady speaking voice. Or, to quote Chairman Nkruma:

"You want to get through to these kids? Then be a Fascist."

*A Fascist. Excellent. I could do this.*

And just as I'm happily dusting off that old brown shirt hung in the back of my closet, Nkruma goes on to elucidate:

"Call their parents. Make them terrified of you."

But I don't want to call their parents. I would far rather invade Abyssinia and make the trains run on time. Hell, I would rather be attacked by my own men and hung naked and upside down. Isn't that what they did to Mussolini? It doesn't sound so bad. Spring is here.

This is the secret of public education. All those hours you think we're sitting around planning classes, preparing materials, grading, and perhaps even considering new innovations in the wonderful world of reaching young minds, we're not. We're holding a telephone receiver in our hand, hoping no one will answer at the other end.

Only Martin can get away with not calling parents. He has secret wells of monkish allure I cannot understand. He *does* things to the students. They listen with jaws dropped. And if they misbehave, three Hail Marys and a flamenco chord. That seems to keep them in line.

But as for the rest of us, calling parents is an important part of our job. And it *is* a job. First of all, if you have classes going as badly as mine, that means quite a few parents to call: in my case, somewhere between forty and fifty. And it's not exactly as if they're waiting by the phone, either. Do you really want to call people at the office to tell them their little Johnny brained little Susie with a bat, and maybe it's time to have a serious talk? No. You need to wait till they get home, and that could be late. And then when you do reach them, that's when the unpleasantness begins.

Let's face it: often the reason why little Johnny is illiterate, obnoxious, and good at braining is because he first learned it at home. Talking to those parents is no treat. And if Johnny didn't learn it at home, if he's slipping away from parents who are kind and at their wits' end, it's even worse. They weep, sometimes, ask you what to do, and you don't know what to do, except to mumble the truth, that kids may get into trouble, but given time and patience, a lot of them get themselves out, but I know the stakes can be pretty serious and it's not much comfort.

The conversation I dread the most, though, is the one where the parent says, "I just don't understand why he's doing so badly this year," and if you have an honest bone in your body, you must respond, "Uh, could be because of me."

No, I don't want to call parents. My life is stressful enough.

.   .   .

"How's Cindy Fernandez doing?" Leon says to me one day.

*Terrific,* I want to say, *all that exercise running in and out of my room, lying to you about me, has put roses in her cheeks.*

"I hand out a quiz," I say, "she tears it up and then accuses me of not giving it to her. I hand out *anything* and she refuses to take it, and then says I haven't given it out. And what we're doing is so easy, just like you told me, other people are getting hundreds. She's getting a zero. What else can I give her?"

He sighs, unsurprised. "You've got to call Mrs. Fernandez."

"Do I have to?" I cry out childishly, because of course I see that Leon is right.

"Try it," he says. "It won't be so bad."

I stumble into the office and announce, "Where do they keep the ninth-grade phone numbers? I've got to call Cindy Fernandez's mother."

Calvin starts cackling. "Cindy Fernandez! I used to chase her around the *room!* Oh, how I *miss* Cindy Fernandez!"

I don't know whether I should try to shake, or revel in, the image of frail Calvin running round and round the room, trying to catch the hefty (but speedy) Cindy Fernandez, whose breasts, frankly, are bigger than his head.

Am I being mean? Thinking of this? Concentrating on the physical when I myself had my struggle with baby fat, the humiliation of it?

Sure I am. So what?

I pick up the receiver and steel myself. "Maybe Mrs. Fernandez should come into the office. Then we can have a meeting or something. One of those intervention meetings, where we all meet and discuss what's wrong? Maybe it'll help."

"No!" cries June, one of the deans. "Don't call Mrs. Fernandez! She's *horrible*. And I don't even want to *talk* with Cindy."

Could it be? Is June—tough June, competent June—also afraid of Cindy Fernandez? Then what chance can *I* possibly have?

June is the kind of woman who has always terrified me. Her surety. Her almost military aura. Nobody has to tell *her* to be a general. It would be like ordering rain to be wet.

It's not her size that gives her so much authority. She is small and slim, smaller and slimmer than I. Maybe it's that she's so aggressively plain. I don't mean that she's ugly, but rather that she has kept herself plain, it seems to me, as a kind of statement. A power statement.

Her narrow lined face is bare of makeup, her pretty golden hair is cut into clownish curls. As for her clothes: it's hardly fashion central in here, but what can you say about her Chef Boyardee–red and Cheeto-orange tie-dyed windbreaker, except that it is so hideous it's got to mean something? There's got to be a secret educational message in a jacket like that.

*So you think it's ugly? Who cares what you think? I've got more important things on my mind than mere aesthetics here. We've got children to educate, out of my way.*

or,

*Yes, I am completely color blind. But tell me. What's so great—so goddamn great—about seeing in color?*

or, since less is sometimes more,

*So you don't like it? Tough.*

Yes, June is tough. She has a mission, and when you've got a mission, a desire not to look like somebody's unfortunate lunchroom accident must seem pretty trivial.

I wish I could learn from June, pick up an authority tip or two. But I don't see how I can. For I have military dyslexia. I'd like to bark out orders, I really would, it's just that I bark differently: it comes out of my mouth like a self-pitying plea for mercy.

Not that it matters, for it turns out we've arrived at the same place.

"Don't call her," June says. "Please. The last thing we want is *her* in the office. It won't accomplish anything! She's impossible. Just ignore her."

"Cool," I say, putting down the phone.

Then Leon walks into the room. "Have you called Mrs. Fernandez?"

"No," I say. "June said I didn't have to."

"Oh, come on," says June briskly. "Give her a call. It won't be so bad."

I glare at her.

*Be a general?*

*How about Benedict Arnold?*

Leon looks at me with gentle fatherly concern. "Well?"

"I can't. Please don't make me."

"I tell you what," he says. "I'll call her, then I'll put you on the phone."

"Okay," I say, bowing my head.

He dials.

I am rescued for the moment.

She's not home.

Cindy, Lucille, Marcy, Charles, and Wilbur are having a debate.

"MOST REDHEADS ARE WHITE!"

"*NO, WHAT ARE YOU TALKING ABOUT? MOST RED-HEADS ARE PUERTO RICAN!*"

"YOU CRAZY? WHITE!"

"*NO! PUERTO RICAN!*"

"WHITE!"

"*PUERTO RICAN!*"

"*LISTEN,*" screams Marcy, in such a passion she half hurls her skinny little body across the desks, "MY AUNT'S A HAIR-DRESSER! SHE OUGHTA KNOW!"

But that's not the end of it.

"*LOOK.* WHAT COLOR IS THE SPANISH TEACHER'S HAIR? RED. WHAT IS SHE? PUERTO RICAN!"

Oh God, I think, sinking my face into my hands, this is so stupid and horrible and boring someone should write a book about it.

*Oh.*

*Oh.*

*Oh.*

*Oh.*

*Oh.*

I *knew* there was a reason I didn't take that census job.

I take up my pen, a rare euphoria suffusing my body with sweet heat.

Someone is going to shout out something else *moronic.*

I feel it.

I *know* it, and I . . .

am ready.

And then one day, I get a letter.

I have just come home from school, and I put my key in the mailbox, and the minute I take out the letter, and see where it's from, waves of all the desire I have taught myself to suppress take me over.

*It's too soon,* I think. *It's nothing.*

*Don't expect anything.*

*Zen. Zen. Zen.*

I open the letter. It is from the Writers at Work Competition in Utah, a competition I have dearly—*forgive me, for competition, as opposed to cooperation, is an evil*—wanted to win. If you win, you get published in *Quarterly West,* an excellent journal. You get $1,500, which, for a poet, is a lot. You get a reading at the Writers at Work conference in July.

Far be it from me to rely on the outside world for validation.

I am a general.

I am also, it turns out, a finalist.

They will let me know if I have won by the end of May.


I walk up the stairs in a daze, in a hot swoon of hope so rich I have to stop on the first landing to catch my breath.

*Oh man. Do I want this.*

And wanting it, I have to stop myself. Wanting is dangerous. Wanting something means you won't get it. Wanting breaks your heart.

I tell myself sternly to rid myself of all desire. It's just a dumb contest, one among many, it doesn't mean anything, most people haven't even heard of it, not that it matters: I won't win anyway. And even if I do win, what difference does it make?

It doesn't matter. I'm not listening.

I have been writing for years. Last September, I began sending out a poetry manuscript to different publishers. Not that I really thought it would be taken. I had heard too many stories of near acceptance, of bitterness and disappointment. You strive—you have to strive—to keep expectations low. Writing is enough. That is what you tell yourself: it is a privilege simply to put the words down and invent a universe. Whether your universe is furnished with comets and constellations, or only with black holes, is un-important.

And then one day, you get a letter.

You write your poems, you slip them in the envelopes. You send them out and then they disappear, like notes tossed into an abyss. That's what it feels like, sometimes. But at least once, someone was standing at the bottom of the abyss. Somebody *saw.*

I sit in the kitchen of my railroad flat, by the window with its view of brick walls and one gallant ailanthus tree, and I stare and stare at that letter, and as I do, as if that paper were alive, it starts inventing things.

It invents the phone call at the end of May, the voice with the flat *A* of the West telling me I have won, and furthermore, *they have never seen such eloquence. . . . Oh God.* This is pure indulgence, far worse than guava pastries, but for this minute, *let me.* Let me imagine it, for it might be the only trip like this I take. I shut my eyes, and the number-seven train unhooks itself from its dull boulevards and slides out of Grand Central Station into the country.

Oh, I will be sorry, I know I will, to have dreamt this dream. But here I go. There's no emergency cord to stop this trip, so I might as well enjoy it. Philadelphia, Washington, Chicago, a ruined warehouse, a boy on a bicycle, the little towns that must be deadly to live in but that I always long for when I glimpse them through the window of a moving vehicle: the one traffic light at dusk, the pharmacy, the pawnshop, the church, the pickup truck, the neon blink of the cheap motel, The Paradise. And if anyone is sitting at the counter, ready to yell how much she hates me, we leave her quickly, because this train is truly a mighty good train, it only picks up passengers with a destination.

I am thinking of the train pulling through the prairie, that flat endlessness of wheat and corn, and I'm thinking, *This is what hope is.* It pulls you through a landscape where nothing seems to change and then it *does* change. The mountains rise up in Colorado, and you are ashamed that somewhere between one cornstalk and another you had almost stopped believing in them. But here they are. The mountains rise up, like a crown, you think, or a set of mad dentures placed upon a tabletop. Their color is like nothing found in a dictionary but halfway between old brick and violets rubbed between the fingertips. So this is where you had been heading. Not the ruined warehouse, and not the Paradise, where the bored clerk rolls another stick of gum into her mouth and announces: *I should know, I'm a ninety-six-year-old motel clerk and I should know!* No. *Here.* Through that distance, air smelling of sage and must, toward the abyss. Which is no abyss at all, it turns out, but a hollow carved out of the ground to cup sound. This is where you had been heading all along.

"ALL RIGHT. ALL RIGHT. *ALL RIGHT.*"

Homeroom. Early yet. I've just draped my coat over the back of my chair and put my newspaper down on the table. It's still relatively quiet, just a sleepy hum of voices beginning, and even Tim has not yet punched Bob, and Bob has not yet punched Tim; I nod a *Hello* to anyone paying attention. That's when June and Tom, unexpected visitors, march into the room. Looking none too happy. Looking, actually, terrifying.

"ALL RIGHT," Tom says. He plants his hands on his hips, sergeant-style, and the class suddenly falls into silence. Amazing. Not a word, not a groan, not a sigh. Waiting.

"SO," says June. She's wearing that jacket again, strutting around like a warden in a woman's prison movie. Any moment now I can see her scooping up Lucille, say, by the front of her shirt and shouting in her face, *So! How are we feeling now, missy??? Not so cocky now, are we?*

And Lucille, weak in June's grip, though she must outweigh her by eighty pounds, just burbling *uhhuhuhuhuhuhuh.*

June folds her arms beneath her breasts and looks out at the room.

"SO. THE NINTH GRADE WANTED THEIR RIGHTS."

"THEIR RIGHTS," says Tom, in a voice dripping sarcasm, and though I have been told that sarcasm doesn't help, it *does:* the students of 9B are sitting there, shoulders back, eyes round, faces impossibly young. Scared. "THEY WANTED THEIR RIGHTS."

"YES." June's voice is even more sarcastic than Tom's now, and June, sarcastic, is even more frightening than June absolutely straight. "I GUESS THEY DID."

"AND LOOK WHAT THEY *DID* WITH THEM."

Tom throws something down.

"THEY DID *THIS*."


"ALL RIGHT. ALL RIGHT."

*I'm back. I can't believe it.*

I thought I had escaped, I really had. But here I am: hands planted on the desk. Eyes looking down. My little bottom glued to the chair.

*P.S. 221. Mrs. Roberts's class.*

*Oh my God.*

"All right," she says.

*Mrs. Roberts.*

Those were the days, back in P.S. 221, when we wouldn't *think* of calling our teachers by their first names. It was always Mrs., unless it was Miss, but it was never—and we liked it that way, at least we couldn't imagine another way—*Imelda*. As in Marcos. *Eva*. As in Braun. It was Mrs. Roberts to you, fools. *Got that? Elizabeth? You? In the back? Stop sniveling. Are you listening? CLASS?*

And now Mrs. Roberts is patrolling the aisles of the fifth-grade classroom, marching slowly up and down on her slim heels, hands planted firmly on her slim waist, nothing on her person daring to jiggle or slip—no roll of the hip, no spare eyelash or strand of hair—*they know the value of discipline, she and her body parts have nothing more to discuss*—and as she goes, she looks into each quivering face of each possible criminal before returning to her desk and folding her hands.

"One of you left the cap off the glue bottle," she says. "Who was it?"

She narrows her eyes. "Oh, *you* know who you are. Speak up."

Silence.

"Well," she says. "It's a nice day, and I'm sure you all want to get out of here, I sure know I do, but we're just going to have to sit here until the Person who left the cap off the glue bottle admits it and Puts It Back On."

Silence. Silence. Silence.

"Maybe you think it's amusing. Maybe you think it's funny. Maybe you think someone *else* will put the glue cap back on. Maybe that's the way you live your life. Let someone else pick up after you. You don't have to be responsible. Not you. Well. Let's see what kind of life you end up living."

Silence. Not a single volunteer. No hoodlum who pulled the cap off the glue bottle for the pleasure of destruction. No sacrificial lambs, no teachers' pets who think they could get away with a crime like that, could be forgiven. No teachers' scapegoats, either. No one.

"I'm waiting," she says. "I'm waiting."

And so she does, not cheating in any way. She doesn't read a book or correct papers. She doesn't file an already perfect nail. She just sits there, gazing at us, so young, so evil, so careless with school property.

We gaze back, shameless, as the afternoon that will soon be gone forever washes its blue upon the panes.

*Did I do it?*

*Was I the one?*

I'm trying to play the scene of the screwing of the glue cap in my mind and even though it happened, or didn't happen, just minutes before, I can't remember. I just can't. She gets in my brain, Mrs. Roberts, she needles it full of holes like a bad case of syphilis. I can't think.

Though I know the truth.

*It was me.*

If not the glue cap, something. It *had* to be. Something.

It was inevitable. There's a whole roomful of things to be done wrong, and some of them *must* be done wrong. By me.

Not that it matters. Draw and quarter me first, I won't confess. To anything.

I lift up my evil, rosy face.

A boy—they are made, after all, of weaker stuff—stifles a laugh.

"So you think it's funny," Mrs. Roberts says. "I tell you what. Come back to me in ten years, Buster, and why don't you tell me then how funny it is?"


And now the heavy snakes of cable fall to the floor with a thud and Tom gazes into each 9B face.

"Someone," he says, "thought it would be funny to disconnect all the computers. Someone in here likes to destroy. Someone thinks there's nothing *funnier* than *destruction*."

*Oh. So that's why it was so quiet in here this morning. It was nice.*

"Now it's not easy to do a thing like this. This is a job for some-one who *knows* computers. Not anyone can do it. It takes skill. And furthermore," he says,

"it takes *hours*.

"And you know what that means? It means somebody *saw*. Somebody *had* to see.

"And that somebody must have talked. They *always* talk. And if somebody talked, that means somebody *heard*. Somebody knows.

"But no one has told us *anything*."

"But how do you know it's *us*?" someone pipes up.

"Oh we know. We *know*."

"Your *rights*," says June, disgustedly. "I am *sick* of your rights. You know, *other* people have rights, too. There are seniors right now applying to colleges. They *need* those computers. They've got to write their entrance essays. But they can't, now, can they? Their whole lives depend on these computers. So what do they have to do? They have to wait to use mine. You should *see* the line of students waiting to use my computer. It's snaking out the *door*."

"I know some of you think this is one big joke," says Tom. "So why aren't you laughing?

"I tell you this: It's not funny. Louis is going to have to spend *hours* of his valuable time reconnecting the computers. And we'll have to pay him. Louis's time does not come cheap!"

"We know some of you know who did this," says June. "You know who committed this act of . . . *disrespect*."

"Yes," says Tom. "Disrespect. And until we find out who it was, the ninth grade will . . ."

He whips out the ultimate punishment.

"Not leave the school for lunch. You will eat lunch in the school cafeteria."

Horror and shock on the student faces.

*Vengeance is mine, saith the Lord.*

# THE NEW YORK MOUTH

*The Paper for the Leaders of Tomorrow . . . Today.*

---

# !!!!!!!!!!!WAR!!!!!!!!!!!

## Unidentified Ninth-Graders Rip Out Computer Cables, Rm. 313

---

## "We Will Find Culprits," Vows Tom

*Reward Offered for Information—Infinite Self-Esteem*

TOM GRIPPING RIPPED-OUT COMPUTER CABLE.

NEW YORK, April X.

Waves of shock swept through the School of the New Millennium today as news of the vandalization of the computers in Room 313 became known. Unknown perpetrators had ripped cables from the computers, necessitating "hours of work" by Louis in order to repair them.

"This was sheer callousness, a wanton act of destruction," June announced. "This is when high-school seniors are applying to colleges, and these computers are needed."

"We don't know who the culprits are," Tom said. "But somebody does. Until the vandals are caught, we have no choice but to keep pulling lunch cards. This is School Property we're talking about. We can't take the destruction of it lying down."

Some other members of the School of the New Millennium have another point of view, however.

"Kids will be kids," said Louis. " Truth is, it took me no more than a couple of hours to rehook the cables. I think perhaps we are overreacting."

Peter Garcia, while surrounded by Tim'n'Bob, Juliet Delacroix, and other 9B students, announced for them all, "I didn't do it. And I don't know who did it, either. Don't you think if I knew who did it I would say something?"

Even Elizabeth, the new ninth-grade English teacher, expressed doubts. "Far be it from me to support the ninth grade," she said. "But do they really have proof that it was a ninth-grade student who did it? That classroom is open after school so anyone can come in and use the computers. If you ask me, the administration is just angry at the ninth grade for being such a pain in the neck so they're expressing their frustration." (continued, page x)

# THE ALLURE OF SCHOOL PROPERTY

*by Elizabeth Gold*

What's the allure of school property? Why its power to make the most laid-back, tolerant, understanding school official morph into a Dickensian, stick-wielding, porridge-denying brute? I know it's bad, *very very bad*, to pull cables out of the computers just for the joy of it. But what about yelling HOMO in class? Isn't that an act of psychological vandalism that could hurt the psyche of a young boy wrestling with his sexual identity? And what about pulling a *Gaslight* on me? *(haha, and if you think you're succeeding, vile harpies from Hell, you're wrong, wrong, dead wrong)* Isn't that vandalism of a sort, too? Yet faced with these crimes, the school administration has proven nothing but understanding. No lunch cards pulled. No accusing an entire grade of an act they didn't necessarily do and then expecting the whole grade to pay for it. No. In the HOMO case, a simple explanation of "learning disability" and "kids will be kids" sufficed, and as far as *Gaslight* goes—this teacher is still waiting for Joseph Cotton to show up.

The School of the New Millennium might say it's different from other schools, more tolerant, loving, familial (I refer you to *King Lear, The Brothers Karamazov*) but in this it resembles any other school in the world. I remember well my days in P.S. 221, which, on the whole, were pretty civilized—that is, of course, unless anyone had the temerity to mess around with school property. I will never forget that lunch period when, sternly instructed not to spill my milk, the School Poltergeist had no choice but to slip into my carton and rebel. The result? Well, they say therapy will help, but my question is, how much?

Though my anthropology is weak, I can only surmise that for schools, certain objects possess a totemic power. Within the body of the Computer lives the Spirit of the Clan. To hurt the Computer is to hurt the Clan. And though, maybe, in some primitive way, this is true, I would hope, if we were as forward-looking as we say, we would set aside old beliefs in the mystic powers of nail parings and voodoo dolls and see our computers, nay, *all* our objects, for what they are: objects, not houses for spirits.

Now some would argue that the real problem is quite simply, money. That schools don't have enough of it, and when a child damages property in that very real way he is damaging the school. But that argument would have more validity if the school spent its money more wisely, on books, for instance, and curriculum development. For say what you like about computers, but in the end they are just tools, like a fork or a hammer. You can use them to do things (like play solitaire, for instance) but they cannot teach you to critique and analyze. Only intelligence, curiosity, patience, imagination, *heart*—can do that. And that is property that can't be bought.

But enough about the sorrows of the ninth grade. I've got problems of my own. You see, back when I was all flush with the promise of the census job, I got this idea that as the ninth grade was rebelling, I could rebel, too. They could make their demands, and I, mine. Important demands. Sensible, even idealistic ones. But demands all the same.

And now Leon wants to talk to me about my letter.

I had written that I could not teach without real books, and enough of them for the students to take home. And, that if they didn't *get* me real books, I would quit.

Was I really planning to quit? Maybe then. But *now?* When spring vacation is so close I can taste it?

Judy and I are sitting in Leon's office. I've never seen him this angry. No longer the loving dad, he is now the mad dad, and I am simply very tired: all those weeks of thrown-away lesson plans and other things thrown-away, a lifetime, it now seems to me, of missed chances and bad diplomacy.

"How can we get books now?" he says. "It's spring. It's too late. And you *have* a book. That writing book. People love that book. You will *use* that book."

"It's incomprehensible," I say. "I already know how to write, and let me tell you: It confuses *me.*"

"Here's a chart about how to write a narrative paragraph. Isn't that great? See how clear it is."

I stick to my guns. He's already angry at me, so I might as well try to get what I want. And despite everything, I know he won't fire me, and as for spring vacation: I have a bus ticket for Washington, D.C., already sitting on my dresser at home.

"Leon, all the research (magic words; educators love *all the research*) about writing always comes up with the same result: Writers read. That is the way. The only way. So if you want me to turn these kids into writers, you have to get me books they can read."

"We have *Call of the Wild*."

Oh God. Wolves, dogs, Yukon. *The Mincemeat*. Of me.

"It's a kid's book. It's been listed in The Standards as a book for middle school. This is high school. How can I teach a kid's book?"

"Elizabeth, it doesn't matter what you teach. In the end, you are not teaching a subject. You are teaching *children*. And you will teach *The Call of the Wild*. A good teacher can teach anything. And *you* will teach *this*."

Resistance is useless. Suddenly I realize this.

I hang my head. Now I understand the expression: I feel the weight of it, as if gravity, in an act of personally motivated vengeance, had no choice but to pull down.

"I'm typing up a lesson plan for you," he says.

"Okay," I say weakly.

"You will start *The Call of the Wild*. Tomorrow."

"But we're just finishing 'The Lottery.' You wouldn't want me to stop before we're done, would you? Then we'd have no *consistency*."

"That's true. Then we will have a quiz about 'The Lottery.' Five questions they can answer. It will give them confidence. It will help their self-esteem. So. What is 'The Lottery' about?"

*Okay, so he's never read "The Lottery." The world is filled with people who have never read it.*

*The prime minister of Uzbekistan, for instance.*

"Well, it's about some villagers, and they have this problem with conflict resolution, and they're not always good at managing their anger, and so they express it by—"

"All right," says Leon, typing away. "After the questions you will give them a mini-grammar lesson. No longer than fifteen minutes, because then their attention strays. Keep them busy. Always busy. How about doing"—he flips through a grammar workbook—"um, punctuation? And then—we'll have some students deliver *The Call of the Wild.*"

I nod, almost tearful.

"You will give them a mini lecture on Man Versus Nature."

*Man versus Nature. Nature red in tooth and claw, ships versus barnacles, sherpas versus yetis, Dorothy versus that tornado . . .*

"Okay," I say.

"This nonsense, this nonsense of all these demands, it's going to be over, isn't it?"

*Sure. Me and Buck (or is it Fang?) are planning to run off to Moosejaw and live off blubber cakes.*

"Yes," I say.

"You're doing a fine job. Really. You should give yourself a pat on the back. I think the kids are settling down. You're making real progress. So don't be so hard on yourself.

"I just have one question to ask you," he continues. "Do you know who tore the cables out of the computers? Did you see anything?"

*See anything? How could I? I was too busy standing on my desk, eyes closed in exultation, screaming them on.*

*Finally doing something together like a family.*

"No. Of course not. This didn't happen when I was around."

I suddenly feel ridiculously protective of the ninth grade. My kids. Sarah, and Peter, and Adam, and Ken, and Erica, and sweet, goofy Tim.

I say, "Are you *sure* it's the ninth grade? It's the technology classroom, lots of people use it. People use it in the morning. And after school."

"Oh we know it's the ninth grade."

"*How?*" I say, but he brushes off my question.

"Damaging property like that," says Leon. "It's bad. It's *very very* bad."

We are having a meeting. It is so strange that in the midst of all this Charter-applying, Teacher-developing, Standard-raising, Voice-expressing, Computer-destroying, Ninth-Grade disciplining, Guava pastry–eating, never mind The Call of the Wilding, we still have time—we *always* have time—for the true purpose of school, which is, I have found out, to have meetings.

This time, with Randolph and his father.

*It has come to our attention that Randolph is not doing his best.*

Well, I wouldn't say that was completely true. As far as yodeling HOMO goes, he is first-rate.

Can you really blame me for resenting Randolph? For introducing into my classroom psychosexual drama? I mean, Vincent tells me this is not the seventies, man, and whatever our sexuality is, it's cool, it's cool, no one gets upset anymore, and maybe that's true, but if it were completely true, if HOMO had all the emotional impact of a word like OKAPI, or GRAPEFRUIT, he wouldn't be yelling it now, would he?

To quote Lucille: Whatever.

How strange it is to see Randolph sitting here. So quiet. So wary. His hands neatly folded, *a boy, really, a little boy,* I think. Randolph has always struck me as a kid with a lot of charisma. He is a handsome boy, with a dark velvety skin the color of Guinness; a boy whose presence, for better or worse, could eat up a room. But next to his father, the Sun God, a man with the world's greatest posture, a brass medallion round his neck depicting—what else?—*Himself—the sun*—Randolph seems shy, diminished, eager for instruction. Even, perhaps, for punishment.

I myself am fighting the desire to worship. To fling myself upon the ground and plead, if not for mercy, then a little bit of a tan.

Elaine stands up. She is one of the special-ed experts. Now that I have been at the school for two months, I have begun to realize how many of our students are classified as special ed. As far as I can figure, people don't fail school anymore because they're dumb or lazy or reckless or ignorant or pissed off or in despair or have their minds on other things or are just plain uninterested. Now the only explanation for failure is, you've got a syndrome. Why else would rational beings—which of course we all are—choose to do badly at something so good for them?

Still, there is a mystery inside Randolph. He's not stupid, far from it. I have noted more than once the quiet eloquence in his eyes. He can even write a nice shapely sentence. Every once in a while he does so.

Elaine tells Randolph what a good guy he is, how full of potential, and a learner, the way every child is.

Randolph sits there, cowed. His father sits there, blazing.

Elaine tells Randolph that she doesn't have his test scores in front of her, but she knows he has a learning disability of some kind. Since she doesn't know exactly what kind of disability he has, she'll just have to take a guess, and as she's talking her mouth moves slower and slower, painstakingly shaping each word as if her lips were coated with wet glue and she were afraid to crack it while it dried.

"They     are     just     beginning     to     do     studies,

Randolph," she says. "They are just beginning to find out How People Learn. And How Many of Us Learn Differently. Not in a *Worse* way. A different way."

Randolph stares, fascinated.

I'm fascinated myself, suddenly aware of how lips and tongue and teeth conspire together to make words.

Grotesque, really.

"One fifth, Randolph! Yes, at least one fifth! That's a lot of people! See the World a Different Way. Not a *Worse* Way. A *Different* Way. Some of those people have been very famous. Have you ever heard of . . . *Michelangelo?*"

Elaine goes on to describe how when some people look at the world, they see a flat, ordered surface but for people like Michelangelo, they see a kind of grid.

"Is that what you see, Randolph?" she says. "I don't have your test scores in front of me, so I'm guessing. It's a grid, isn't it?"

Randolph looks stunned, whether in relief because the truth is out or just because he's stunned, I cannot say.

I'm stunned, too.

*A grid? Is that really what he sees? A grid? What kind of a grid? A barbecue grill? A map of Manhattan? He looks at me and sees not eyes, nose, mouth, but . . . but . . . a grid?*

Is that why he wants to yell Homo?

Now I know what I've done wrong, for I have always talked to Randolph at normal speed.

For example: RANDOLPH! RANDOLPH! *RANDOLPH!*

He seemed to have no trouble understanding me, but then again, when you're hampered by seeing everything as flat and ordered maybe I just *thought* he understood me. Maybe I was confused.

Sharon, the special-ed teacher, quietly makes a suggestion. "Um. . . . have you thought of giving him. . . . Ritalin?"

At this Randolph's father explodes.

"NO! No drugs! *No drugs!* There is nothing *wrong* with this boy! He just needs to concentrate, that's all!" He glares, at us, then at Randolph.

Who can blame him? A group of well-meaning white people, members of the race that brought the world the Tuskegee Experiment. *No.* We're not going to pump our drugs into his boy. I wouldn't want someone to pump drugs into my boy, either. Even so, I must admit that Randolph does have a little problem with attention span. He can manage *HOMO,* but *HOMOSEXUAL,* with its extra syllables, is beyond him.

Now Tom is looking at Randolph. "How'd you do last marking period?" he says, gently, firmly, man-to-man. "You fail everything?"

"No," snaps Randolph, insulted. "Not *everything.*"

"Good," says Tom, pleased. "What did you pass?"

"Gym," says Randolph.

Even his father laughs.

Oh, it is a sad thing, a very sad thing. Randolph has been sent from school to school as others scramble for solutions. For what, no one really knows. Something that happened in the privacy of his house, in the darkest knots of his brain. *Or not. Or not.* You could explain this till the cows come home, you could milk them and roll wheels of Gouda in hot red wax, you could meet about the cows, and the milk, and the cheese, and still. Here it is. The mystery. I'm thinking about this, as the meeting ends, and I stand to go, and June suddenly grasps Randolph's hands and looks hard into his eyes.

"Randolph," she says. "You're a leader. *I know.* I see the way kids talk to you. Whenever there's something going on, you're in the middle of it. You make things happen. You're in the know. I'm not accusing you of anything. I know *you* wouldn't do anything wrong. But surely you must have heard something. So tell me: *Who vandalized the computers?*"

"It's not fair!" says Eric Antonelli. "It's not fair, it's not fair, it's not fair!"

It is during one of the breaks between classes, and the ninth grade is wandering around the halls, talking about what else—the Computer Imbroglio. The lectures continue. The silence continues. No one is admitting anything, even if there were someone in the room with something to admit. But lunchtime in the basement of the School of the New Millennium, beneath the portrait of the smiling dead teacher, is wearing them down.

I look at Eric and the little group clustered around him. Courtly Ahmed, just moved from Pakistan; the two grinds, Mona and Nadia, with their thick glasses and head scarves; Erica Reynolds; silent Arden; Vincent Daly. I can't see any of them doing this. Even Vincent, who enjoys trouble. But not this kind of trouble. He's a loudmouth, a cutup, an exhibitionist; stealthy destruction is not his style.

"Sorry," I say. "You know this has nothing to do with me."

Of course they know that. That's why they've chosen me to complain to. They sense my indifference to school property.

I'm still steaming about that spilled carton of milk. It was an *accident*.

But Eric's not letting it go. How could he? This is injustice and he's not the sort of boy to take injustice lightly. "Can't you do something?"

I sigh. "Eric," I say, "I know it's not fair. But that's the way it is. You're learning something. When someone acts like an idiot, the group has to pay for it. That's what happens in this world. The innocent get hurt. So you have to do something about it. You have to figure out a way of policing yourselves."

What an asshole.

I'm referring, of course, to myself.

I mean, what story am I living in? "The Lottery"?

Yes, it's true. They are paying for Cindy Fernandez's big mouth and her mean mother and the pressure to get the school up to standard so it will get and keep its charter. They are paying for every failing grade and every HOMO and every Walkman and every time a boy tries to pushpin his fellow students to the bulletin board.

But I don't see why they should. It is, as Eric says, not fair.

It's gotten so bad in 9B I'm afraid to go in. When homeroom is supposed to start, I'm still hanging out in the hall like a juvenile delinquent. If I had hubcaps to steal and a rumble to join, I'd be A-OK. Instead I have to walk into the room and pretend to be Officer Krupke.

How in the world did this happen?

What can I say?

It's not fair, it's not fair.

It's gotten so bad in 9B that sometime between the ninth-grade Town Meeting and the Computer Incident, the administration, without either asking or telling me, has disappeared Ricardo Silva. Not in the Argentine sense. More of a witness protection kind of thing. I still see him around the halls, usually looking sullen but sometimes small. We always pretend we don't know each other. Someone figured out I just couldn't handle him and I needed to stay till June, so they pulled him out, gave him a new identity, and plunked him into Louis's class, where he sits, not so much learning science but drinking in Louis's air of benign but stern fatherliness.

Maybe that's what he needs. Maybe that's more important than topic sentences, than fractions.

It is better this way, no doubt, and many a female teacher—he is hell on the female teachers—would envy me, if they knew. I tell no one, afraid if I do I will break the spell of the absence of Ricardo Silva.

So. No complaints, but still. How can I tell Eric to police his classmates?

If I can't do it, how can he?

Why should he, anyway?

Peter Garcia is looking for something.

"Wait a second," he says, flipping through his notebook, papers flying everywhere, "it's here somewhere."

Maybe it is. I know this kind of notebook. It holds many fragments of secret treasures: a doodle of a face, a sarcastic aside, a phone number, even an algebraic equation, scrawled, as is only proper, in the dog-ear of a page. And it lets go of an equal number of fragments: like the homework one did last night, for instance. In a life of margins and headings, one needs a certain sangfroid to possess a notebook like that.

And Peter Garcia has it. He is calm, unhurried, flipping through his pages. Only a few have been hooked onto the binder's rings. As for the rest . . . he likes movement. He likes that moment when he leaps from the skateboard and if only it went on long enough, it would be flying, instead of a jump.

"Oh well," he says, with a shrug and a smile, shutting the notebook. "Guess I lost it. Have to do it again."

God, this kid, this kid, my most verray, parfit gentil knight, with his baggy army fatigues and his dark eyes that miss nothing. Could I possibly like him more? Is there something wrong with me that I am completely reliant on a fifteen-year-old boy for my protection? Shouldn't it be the other way around?

And shouldn't I be scolding him gently about his notebook? Pointing out how his lack of organization created twice the work?

How a little bit of planning and attention to detail is really worth the time and will help him prepare for college days ahead?

I should.

But how can I? I love Peter Garcia's notebook. I love the little monster drawings. I love the semi-thoughts scribbled in pencil. I love how his mind is somewhere else: in spring, in a moment of wheely flight, or in Middle Earth, having an adventure.

Yes, every piece of paper that swirls behind him is one more sign of subversive inner life: God bless that life.

Listen, Peter. I knew someone once who had a notebook like that. I knew her well.

I was there when her eighth-grade English teacher couldn't stand it anymore, and grabbed the notebook out of her hands, turned it upside down, opened it up, and let the papers go everywhere.

And I was there when she had to get on her hands and knees and crawl after those papers, while the teacher gave her a lecture on neatness and her classmates cackled their heads off.

But *I* wasn't laughing, Peter.

How could I laugh? I was the one on my hands and knees.

And now I'm gazing at Peter's notebook. Is it possible, could it be, that my old notebook spawned other notebooks, each one stubborn in its resistance to order and its love of the flyaway? And if that were true, what other miracles could I expect?

Not that class 9B is where I am expecting them to happen.

Every day I fight the urge to surrender. To jump up and say, *Okay, okay, you win. There are more of you than me and you are so much younger than me, and cuter than me, and cooler than me, and of course much smarter than me, you wear nicer clothes than me, you smoke more cigarettes than me, you have more friends than me, you dance better than me, you have more sex than me, you eat more Big Macs than me, you have far better, less antique, thus improved, ever-onward taste in music than me,* and having waved my white flag I could just lay my head on the floor and Lucille could put down her copy of *Chicken Soup for the Teenager's Soul* and rest her victor's boot on my skull, and from that position I could tell them to turn to page 94 and would they please do exercises A, B, and C?

Something holds me back. Perhaps the fear that Lucille is, after all, a heavy girl, and she might grind her heel in with more force than would be pleasant.

Instead, barricaded behind my desk, I persist in saying in a loud yet trembling voice, " On page 94 the instructions say—"

"No shit, Sherlock! We can read the instructions! What's the matter, you think we can't fucking read that ourselves?" Marcy screams.

At this, suddenly, Zuleika snaps.

Zuleika. She sits on Marcy's side of the room, but she wishes me no harm. Zuleika, with the little giggle, and those odd triangular eyes that seem to fill up sometimes, for no particular reason, with adolescent tears.

She now grips the table and glares at Marcy. "What has she done to you?" she says. " Nothing. So why are you doing this? If she doesn't explain something, you complain. And if she *does* explain, you complain. She can't win, don't you see that? She just can't win."

This is bold. Bolder, even, than Peter Garcia. Peter has always been happy to go his own way, but Zuleika is a team player. And simply by sitting on Cindy and Lucille and Marcy's side of the room, her team is their team. And now she's broken the rules.

What a strange look is on Zuleika's face. She's angry all right, but not, primarily, at Marcy.

She's angry at herself: How could she have done this? Actually defend me? This isn't what she had planned to do. It's just that somehow—she couldn't help it. How could she be so weak and impulsive? To feel what she felt, and let herself give in to it?

She shakes her head, but too late. The damage is done. It has happened again, surrender to something more seductive, sometimes, than chocolate or boys or the urge to suddenly start screaming on the sidewalk at the top of her lungs, that terrible desire that came over her, despite everything, to do good.

Sometimes, when I see the boys wrestling with each other out in the hall, I have a moment of distant compassion, as if I were a kindly angel on a TV show, concerned but unaffected by what happens down below. Is this what Leon means by love? No dates, no valentines, certainly no champagne, nothing Cole Porter would ever write songs about. But something.

*What are they doing here?* I think.

Oh, there's been a mistake, a terrible mistake, a chronological slippage of muscle and bone, and these boys shouldn't be here. Not here. They should be sailing down the Mississippi or fighting wars or killing whales or serving as copy boys or architecture apprentices. They should be doing things and making things, and even finding out that not every adult is a fool or desperate. Or both.

Where they shouldn't be is sitting in some place hour after hour being told that they are the Leaders of Tomorrow when 999 chances out of 1,000 they probably are not.

What a terrible thing to think. Condemning them at this moment to unleaderness, a lifetime of it.

But I don't mean it unkindly. Quite the opposite.

Jacob wrestled with an angel. Not that I want those boys—since I'm playing the angel here—to wrestle with me. But in their bodies, I see that kind of longing, to launch themselves into an empty universe and have contact, to shape things, to make their mark.

Yet there is no empty universe. There is no way to launch themselves. There is just a very narrow doorway, entered by studying for a math test, and then another one, and another one, and summer school, if it has to be that way, and summer school again, though despite the *can-do* speeches—ignorant they may be, stupid they are not—they know the kind of leadership we're trying to pump them up to commit is beyond their ken.

When Mark Twain was a youth, he studied the river. That river bedazzled him, and it broke his heart.

But who cares about rivers anymore, or angels, for that matter?

Let's tell them instead one more time that smoking is bad for them, and reading is good.

That should be enough.


About a week after my meeting with Leon, as 9C is drawing to its close, I hear a knock on the door. It's easier to hear knocks on doors these days; all that lecturing has taken some of the stuffing out of the kids.

It's Judy, accompanied by three twelfth-grade boys pushing a trolley of books.

*The Call of the Wild.* Well, I've been ready for it.

"Just put them on the table," I say. "Thanks."

The students of 9C watch quietly, grateful for any entertainment, as Judy's assistants unload and stack the books in neat piles.

"There are a few more in the storeroom, if you need them," says Judy.

"I think we've got enough."

I continue with my lesson. I say nothing about the piles of

books, and my students don't ask. Somehow, it's what I had expected.

As the class is ending, though, I turn to some of the nicer boys and say, "Alan? David? Ahmed? Will you help me put these books in the cabinets?"

And so they do. How cooperative these boys are, how pleasant and personable, out of the confines of class. Even Alan, who whiles away most of the period, day after day, by drawing pictures of guns. For this moment it is hard to believe he has ever heard the call of that wild. He is smiling, they all are. They like to do something as practical and helpful as picking up books and putting them away. It is good to use their young bodies for something as sensible as this.

Nobody opens a copy, nor asks me why the books appeared and why we are busy shutting them away.

And that's the end of it. I knew it would be.

I have decided, and my decision is final. There is no way I'm teaching *The Call of the Wild*. Leon can't make me. Furthermore, I don't really think he's interested in making me. I have a feeling he cares no more about this book than any other. I could be teaching *Debbie's Body Parts and Their Adventures* if I could prove that her many many partners were highly multicultural.

I have figured out how this school works. It truly is like a family: one of those sitcom families where the inept dad intones something and the kids humor him and then go off and do whatever they want, or at least, what they can get away with.

I have heard even Nkruma say, *Yes, every child is a learner, every child is one to be reached,* and then, as he's sitting down to call one more parent, whisper to me: "Don't mention this to Leon, but just invent some really fun project and say people can work on it or not. The good ones will do it, a few of the others who could go either way will begin to join them, and as for the rest. . . ." He shrugs.

The assumption is that Leon won't notice. Or will forget. Running a school, even a small one, is not easy and requires tons of paperwork. It's distracting. He can't keep every conversation in his mind.

Or perhaps, he just has a short attention span.

May I suggest . . . *Ritalin?*

Whatever the reason, I know the dogfight over *The Call of the Wild* is over. It was over before it even began. And if I have to spend the rest of the year scraping up xeroxes and trying to force kids to read "The Necklace" in *The Language of Literature*, hell, if I have to read them "The Necklace" out loud, even if it is at the top of my lungs, that is what I'm going to do.

Is this a victory?

Not really. But it doesn't matter. *The Call of the Wild* has gotten under my skin the way computers never could. I know what Leon says, but I don't believe it. If I'm going to give those kids something to read, not any old thing will do. Does Leon really think this? How cynical can you get?

How can I teach my students that literature is bereft of meaning? That it is simply an instrument to improve vocabulary for the SATs?

Maybe it can be done, but sorry. Not by me.

This is an age of big questions, fourteen, fifteen, and I suppose, for some of my students, seventeen. And I respect those questions, that is what I *do* respect. How can I then just talk about any old thing, just because it is convenient?

Ever since I had that attack of Smugitis, standing there with Eric Antonelli, out in the hall, I find myself conversing with him in my head. Things being what they are, I can't say I'm sorry to him face-to-face. Sorry for what? Being an adult, and thus, an idiot?

Still, when I see how those dark blue eyes of his suddenly shift to a rainy gray, what I long to do is say the unsayable: *Eric, you better work on that thin skin of yours, and fast.*

*Listen, kiddo,* I'm telling him in my head, as we stroll up the cortex and make a quick left to sit in a shady lobe. You want to know the way of the world? *This* is the way of the world. I know they tell you that you will get what you want. *Just work for it.*

But what I want to say is, yes. Maybe. No. Or in a form so baroque you can no longer recognize it as something you once asked for.

It can drive you mad. Wanting things. Not getting them. Not knowing if you will ever get them. The years can seem so long sometimes.

*Listen.*

This is what you must do: Study patience. And wait.

Wait longer.

Learn to recognize how things take on different colors and shapes, like clouds that turn themselves in a moment from frying pans into rhinoceroses. Just be careful you notice the change before you grab the handle and light a match.

Read *Beauty and the Beast.* Yes, I know. A girl's story. Read it anyway. Read it again.

Fortitude, Eric.

And don't let them fool you: Being a leader is not the great adventure. But to be a soldier of faith, kiddo, and to keep your eyes open: now *that* is *something*.

Meanwhile—and sometimes it seems as if that is all there is—go about your business.

And learn the art of subterfuge. The art of silent and stubborn refusal. You don't have to cooperate. You just have to give the appearance of cooperating. And then you wait. And you wait. And you wait. Adrift, perhaps, in the eyes of the outside world.

Let them think this.

For you know better. You have, buried within you, as if you were an iceberg, the cold fire of your secret plans.

"How's *The Call Of the Wild* going?" Leon asks me, sometime the next week.

"Great. Great."

"Good. I knew everything would work out."

And so it has.

interludes

Look, I *did* try. To love the children, I mean.

Not in that head-tilt, oh-so-sensitive-I-really-care-about-you way. That would be yucky.

Not for me that look of solemn concern, the compassion gig, that oozy feeling you get when forced to deliver—or receive— words of Tough Love or Validating Love or . . .

whatever.

No, give me love as ambush. The moment that sidles in and glances sidelong, cracks a joke, sleepily moves up to untangle a tendril of hair: give me the lull, the love that stumbles in like Elijah, in disguise. This is what I want: the mystery.

Not that this is what I had in mind with 9A, 9B, and 9C.

*"Hey, I love you, class. I really, really, do."*

*"We love you, too, man."*

But I did try to love them, in some fashion, anyway. Honest. There is too much Good Girl in me, believe it or not, not to try it. She's in there, hair neatly brushed, waiting for her gold star. My only problem is, I can't decide if I want to make love to her or throttle her.

Whatever. Let's say that if love is a kind of listening, a paying of close attention, then, yes, at times, I did listen that carefully. But what was I supposed to do with what I heard?

When Charles, for instance, looked up from his hip-hop magazine and said, "Why don't we study something we're interested

in? Something *real*? Something like this?" what was I supposed to
say? The truth? That despite what he thought, there were plenty
of people in that room (including me, *especially* me) who had no
interest whatsoever in what he was reading?

Besides, what difference does it make if you have decided that
you're interested in this, only this? Does this mean I should design
a curriculum based on wrestling and Chicken McNuggets?

And who ever said that pop music, for God's sake, is real? Is
that what it's about? Then why would anybody listen to it?

It is a dream, Charles, like all the other dreams: a dream of
guns. And violence. And swagger. And girls—infinitely willing,
mindless girls. It is a world stripped of all ambiguity, where the
choices you've got are two: poverty and degradation or living
large, a life of greedy splendor: champagne to guzzle, Mercedes
to be chauffeured in, Armani to flaunt, and don't forget the
chains: not the ones people were once forced to wear but new
ones, chains of gold, though chains all the same.

Sometimes it seems snobbish of me to judge. I am, after all,
pro-dream. A little bit of glamour provides a refreshing alternative to those rote things the adults say: *Don't smoke. Don't do drugs.
Don't have sex, especially unprotected sex. Do your homework. Listen to
your father . . .* all those messages programming you to live not
large but small. Can I blame Charles for yearning for escape?

Still, if dreaming means that you don't pay attention to anything else—including alternative dreams, ones that you persist
you are not interested in, even though you don't even know they
exist—then I've got to argue with it. Because you spin a dream,
and after a while, the dream is so alluring, so much better than
taking out the garbage and doing your homework, that it seems

like the dream is dreaming you, and you are the one who is in-substantial, a ghost.

So forget the real. I am the one who decides what's real. Call me your Education Dominatrix here. I decide. I, I. You have no choice—I really love you, man—but to obey.

"Can't you just tell them," my father says, once a good boy himself, "this is for their own good?"

Try that with an adolescent and see how far you'll get.

So. Forget their own good. Say I listened. Listened hard, at least once. To the way the events and surroundings of an adolescent's immediate world can so overwhelm him he can imagine no other. I listened, and I decided, as best I could, to offer them a key.

It was soon after the Amadou Diallo verdict. The police had been acquitted, the protesters were protesting, yet here, in the School of the New Millennium, the future leaders of the future felt nothing at all. Or so it seemed to me, but I was wrong.

It's not easy to think of a time when Cindy Fernandez was simply that big, eloquent, self-dramatizing girl in the back of 9B. A time before she was my enemy. But one morning, she slammed her book shut and began to speak, and my first experiment in *real* began.


"The thing is," she says, "it was an all-white jury. What do you expect?"

The roar of 9B comes to a stop.

I hoist myself up on the desk, and a vision of the teacher I'd like to be—I've just started, I think I can do it, to become a kind of poor man's Nkruma, smart, sexy, idealistic, inspiring, the stuff of which movies are made—suddenly bobs up and down in me like a worm in a bottle of mescal.

"Actually, Cindy, it wasn't an all-white jury. It was mixed. What do you think that might mean?"

Ricardo puts down his can of soda.

"How come there was no *Spanish* on the jury?"

"The jury was paid off," says Wilbur. "There's no way the government was going to let those cops go to jail."

And they're off. I let them go. Let them vent their fear and anger and grief and resentment and paranoia. It's not for me, not now, to talk about how the government (whatever government it is we're talking about) didn't have to pay the jury off: not when good money—and the police union did have good money—bought good lawyers. That's not what they want to hear. It's too complicated. I have nothing, no material at hand, to back it up. So I sit and listen. But meanwhile I'm thinking that to boil down everything to identity politics is missing the point. It's part of the point, but no way is it the only one.

It doesn't matter though. I am so relieved that they are reacting, that we are actually having a conversation, that I don't care if what they are saying is accurate or not. I can care about that later. Now my students are actually talking about something going on in the larger world, and I think that I should make use of this. I should not throw this passion away.

After school is out, I knock on Rachel's door, and I tell her the idea that came to me in about five minutes of fevered idealism.

She is so gracious. She doesn't laugh at me, the new kid in town. Quite the opposite. She likes my idea. She thinks it might even work. Truth is, she tells me, she's been so sick about events, and about the passivity and cynicism of a lot of her students, that she really had wanted to do something. Maybe this?

Long into the evening, Rachel and I sit and talk about our plans for a new curriculum. Of course it is impossible; and maybe, even as we're talking, we see that. You can't institute a new curriculum past the middle of the year. Finding materials, putting them together, seeing how one class coordinates with another . . . this all takes time, and it's better if the planners aren't working in emergency mode.

Still, we try. We come up with a Human Rights curriculum. All the teachers in the humanities cluster would participate. Miriam teaching economics, Nkruma and Tom history, Rachel and Martin and I teaching writers who had written about, or fought for, or even been punished for, their struggle for justice. "I have a friend who works for Amnesty International," I say. "Maybe he could help."

I tell Rachel about this story I've been reading about in the paper. A group of law students and journalists in Illinois investigated state death row cases. They went over the texts of the trials and what they discovered was so much incompetence— witnesses not called, evidence not submitted, in one trial, the court-appointed lawyer actually falling asleep—that when they handed the findings in to the governor he decided to suspend the death penalty. A conservative governor, a death penalty governor, mind you—a decision such as that must not have been easy.

"I'm going to bring those articles in to my class," I say. "I need to show them that yes, they're right, bad things happen, especially if you're poor. But you *can* do something about it, if you make an effort. Isn't that better than thinking everything is some vast conspiracy organized to keep you down, so why bother?"

Rachel is excited. "The passivity of our students," she says. "It drives me mad. They complain, God knows they complain, but do something, anything? That would be so uncool."

"We're going to *make* them be smart," I say. "Those men on death row were trapped by poverty—but not only poverty. By ignorance. But we're going to teach our students that people can change things. We're going to teach them about action!"


And now it's Monday morning, and Marcy looks up from the article I have so proudly tracked down and xeroxed and handed out.

"I don't care," she says.

Heat enters my face.

"You don't care? They saved people's lives."

"Big deal."

Over on the other side of the room, Peter and a few other kids are trying to read and concentrate. But as for the rest: the hitting is beginning; and the screaming; and the imbibing of the carbonated beverage. My head begins to pound.

The day stretches ahead; two more classes of people not caring. How foolish of me to think they might. How hokey, old-fashioned, idealistic to think I could actually inspire someone. But I'm not quite ready to let it go.

"Don't you realize how remarkable this is?" I say. "What they did? Simply by carefully going over case after case? Those people saved lives. They changed a man's mind. They challenged a system. This is *big*."

"They were just doing it to feel good."

Lucille glares at me. "Those prisoners," she says. "A lot of them are black, right? It just goes to show. A black man can't get a break in this country. You're black, you go to prison. Nothing new."

"No," I say. "The point is, that if you're poor and uneducated, you've got fewer options. It's easier to get in trouble. And you don't know your rights when you do. But that can be changed, and people can work to change it."

"Let's talk about Amadou Diallo," says Lucille. "What are you going to do about him?"

"What do you mean?"

"I mean," she says, "what are *you* going to do?"

"Well, I can go to a demonstration, and—"

"I don't care about that demonstration shit. I mean what are you, *Elizabeth*, individually, going to do?"

"Me? Alone? I can't do anything alone. Protest takes place as a group, that's what it does, one person can't make change, many people have to work for change—"

"You can do nothing," she says. "You admitted it. You can do nothing."

I find myself yelling. I don't know which class. I don't know which hour. All I know is, the ones who aren't hostile are bored, and the other ones are busy enjoying the usual amusements: groping, chewing, listening to music, throwing things on the floor, banging the desks around, howling, playing on the computers, ululating a *HOMO* or two:

"YOU DON'T *CARE* ABOUT AMADOU DIALLO. DON'T TELL ME YOU *CARE*. IF YOU CARED, YOU'D CARE ABOUT *THIS*. IT'S THE SAME. THEY'RE INNOCENT PEOPLE. THEY WERE ON DEATH ROW. PEOPLE *SAVED* THEM. SO DON'T TALK TO ME ABOUT AMADOU DIALLO. DON'T TELL ME YOU CARE. YOU *DON'T*. YOU JUST CARE BECAUSE HE WAS ON TV."

I'm not saying this was *nice* behavior on my part. I'm just saying this is what happened.

And then, as I'm standing there, in the middle of 9A, harried, desperate, with no idea what will be the next word out of my mouth, a silence comes into the room.

Leon.

Strange how this remains after everything else has gone: fear of the principal. The students settle back into their chairs, they practically tug their forelocks.

"What's going on here?" he says pleasantly.

What's the correct answer?

*A. a reenactment of the Fall of Saigon. B. a reenactment of the explosion at Krakatoa. C. A reenactment of the cyanide moment at Jonestown. D.* . . .

"We're just trying to read an article," I say, weakly.

"Let's see what it's about," he says, in that same mild, slow, pleasant voice, as if he knew, even though I was stubbornly refusing to accept it, that there was a grid, in me. "Let's read for a little bit."

And they do. I watch them do it. Turn their faces down, flick their eyes over the page. Remarkable.

Leon starts to teach my class. Partly I'm glad. I am tired, and it's nice to have a break. But I also know I have lost face completely, and Leon is not helping.

"Louise?" he says. "Would you like to read this passage, please?"

She reads it, and he asks her a question, and she answers it.

School, I think. The dipped eyelids, the raised hands, it's like some living tableau played out on an old battleground, Gettysburg, for instance. School. And why Leon can do this, ask a question and have them answer it, and I cannot, well. I'm sure there is a logical explanation:

*I am bad. I am very very bad.*

"This is called Critical Reading," Leon says, in his slow pedantic voice, and I hang my head like one of those sullen loser students who sit in the back of the room, decorating their notebooks with pentagrams, and I think, *Critical reading? And what was I doing? The hula?*

I glower, as only a loser student knows how to do, but say not a word.

"Well?" says Leon. "Why do you think this happened in Illinois?"

Maurice opens his eyes.

Who knew Leon had powers? For Leon is a Prince. Leon can awake Maurice without even the intermediary of a kiss.

"It's Giuliani, man, " he says. "It's goddamn Giuliani."

Far be it from me to mention that Giuliani is the mayor of New York, and we've been talking about the governor of Illinois. That would be so picky.

If Leon notices, he gives no sign. He looks at Maurice and nods his head. The student response has been validated.

Then the ghost of the clapper shudders in the ghost of the bell, and the students gather up their books in quaint orderly fashion and file out of the room.

One more class to go. I watch them leave, and I take a breath, and I go out into the hall.

Leon is waiting for me. I prepare myself for chastisement.

"You must think less of your own suffering," he says, "and more of the suffering of the children."

I just stare at him. I can think of nothing to say.

A few days later, Nadia, a Pakistani girl, small and slight in her loose trousers and head scarf, stays after class to talk to me.

"That article you gave us?" she says. "That was really interesting. I'd love to read more."

"That was just supposed to be the beginning," I say. "I was already working on getting someone from Amnesty International here, and maybe, I thought, we could adopt a prisoner and write letters for a release, and, and, I was going to do literature, of course, and—"

"That sounds great," she says.

"Maybe it is," I respond, petulantly. "Maybe it's not. All I know is, I can't do it. A day like the one when we read the article? No thank you. You see how the students responded. I'm not going through that again."

She shakes her head and sighs. "The people here, they're unbelievable. They have rights that people in my country would go to jail for. But what do they do with them? Nothing."

Later I will think about Nadia, and what it must be like, to move through the halls in this foreign place in her shroud of ancient modesty. Perhaps I don't look hard enough to see the child in her or remember how painful it is to always feel like a stranger. It's easy enough to be attentive in retrospect. But perhaps, for Nadia at least, it is true. I don't think hard enough about the suffering of the children. Or what suffering can do to you.

Despite what some think, it doesn't always make for improvement.

I sigh, too, relieved at least, to have this quiet, sane moment when I am reminded that after all, there is some kindness in me. And then, even this early on, I begin the process. I give it up, I give her up, I give them all up, as I must.

It is spring. Flowers blooming, *check,* breezes blowing, *check,* lads and lasses at play, *check check check.* And here's Sarah Patel, walking toward the subway and then home, long hair shining like water, eyes dark pools, no slouch as far as spring is concerned.

*Fat,* she thinks. *I am just so fat.*

It is with her almost all the time, this fat, like some kind of religious garment you are forbidden to take off, even while showering or making love, *not* that she would make love, she is not ready for that, and besides, when you make love, you have to take off your clothes, and she is just so—

Now, walking down the street, past the crowds of smoking, fried-food-eating people, she contemplates the horror of her clothes: the T-shirt tugging over the little breasts she is not sure she even wants yet, the pants getting tighter and tighter and . . .

If she were not fat, if she were not expanding and taking up more room than was allotted her, if she were not so selfish about this kind of thing, Helen would still like her.

Helen. Her best friend. Her only friend, really, in this new school. It was Helen's mother who convinced Sarah's mother that she should apply here. And she got in, and the school is nothing like they said, and Helen suddenly won't talk to her anymore, she walks down the hall with her new friends, and the *look* she gives Sarah, like she's some kind of fatal disease, only a disease that is as embarrassing as it is dangerous, she looks Sarah up and down and says nothing, but one of her newly plucked brows rises and she laughs, and she whispers something in the ear of her new friend, and then the new friend looks at Sarah and laughs, and Sarah knows the reason, it is just because, if she were not so fat, perhaps it wouldn't be awful to be seen with her. You have to be careful, who you're seen with.

If only she weren't so hungry all the time.

*Tomorrow,* Sarah thinks. *One piece of dry toast, one glass of water, one yogurt. Strawberry? Blueberry.*

Fat was like an attitude. You could change it, and with it your luck. All you had to think was, *I can do it!* and then you could.

She just wishes she were there already.

The breeze suddenly goes cold, like a souvenir of the month before, when it was winter, and she thought—such was her bad attitude—that it would never be warm again, and Sarah shudders, and pauses for a second to disentangle her hair. And catches a glimpse of herself in a store window.

*Oh,* she thinks, before she can stop herself. *Beautiful.*

Her lips curve up at the treacherous thought—how could *she* be beautiful?—and as she is smiling, she feels something. Not so much a touch but the idea of a touch. As if someone were staring at her, a stranger in a subway, a stranger who couldn't decide if he meant you good or harm.

"Hello?" says Sarah Patel, watching her beautiful lips moving. "Hello?"

No one answers, but still she feels it. She turns around.

"Is anybody there?"

It is one day or another day, sometime after the first energetic push of the student rebellion, and the general chaos has died down a little. Some of the students have figured out that if I am not better than your average teacher, I'm not necessarily worse. And for some of them, I might be better, who knows? Whatever it is, a lot of them, today, at least, have figured out that too much of a good thing—continual noise and hostility, for instance—even that could become a tired old thing. And weirdly enough, also, that I'm flexible in my behavior: be nice to me, I'll be nice to you.

The class is scribbling away at some pointless activity. They're all going at it. The opposition, led by Peter Garcia. The leaderless neutral parties sprinkled about the room. Even Marcy, even Lucille, and while Wilbur is not doing it, at least he is quietly asleep. The quiet is most pleasant.

Even Cindy Fernandez is doing the work. I don't know how it happened. She picked up her pen, and as if hypnotized, she began to write.

Why is it that these teenagers look like children when they write? Even Cindy, with that big, womanly face of hers. Remove the opposition from it, and it is still a child's face. As if the effort of putting words down makes you too tired for arguments. Or that listening to a voice, any voice, inside you, softens you up.

And then she looks up, startled.

How could this be? She has been writing, doing it all: words, commas, sentences. Without even spending much effort.

She puts down her pen.

"Oh my God!" she screams. "I just thought of something! What a boring life it is," says Cindy Fernandez, "to be a cat!"

may
**boys and girls together**

## WORD OF THE DAY

frugal *(adjective)* frugality *(noun)* frugally *(adverb):* careful in spending or using resources

Use each version in a sentence.

Damn I hate your frugality.
Why do you act so frugal?
He's so frugally.

Fads sweep the high school like a computer virus, or rather those mysterious sties that suddenly appear on one boy's eyelids and then another before vanishing again. For a while, among the white girls, anyway, it's eye glitter, or stickers pasted on the outer corners of the eyes—Erica Reynolds coming in wearing little photos of—who else?—Buffy the Vampire Slayer. Then suddenly rubbery T-Rex hand puppets appear—given out at McDonald's—I want one, I confess. But why be a follower? Even a teacher can be a trendsetter. Calvin has begun bringing to school jugs of gelatinous Asian sweets, little tubs of fruit-flavored jellies one unpeels the silver foil off of and then sucks down—a soothing, slippery slide down the tongue—and suddenly everyone, kids and teachers alike, is sucking down—in the halls, even in class. "Hey, Calvin!" Rachel whispers, sticking her head into Calvin's room, where he paces, too nervous to sit, surrounded by snack foods and math, the best stuff, the best stuff, on earth, "you got any more of those—you know—those little fruit thingies?"

"I'm out! I'm out! I'll have to go down to Chinatown to get another stash."

Then one day I come to school wearing my candy necklace.

I love my candy necklace.

Strangers smile at me when I wear it, no matter how grouchy I feel, but how can I feel grouchy, wearing my candy necklace? It is so light, so cheap, so goofy, so actually, believe it or not, flattering: its bright pastels look good around my throat. Oh, I *love* my candy necklace. You won't catch any Captains of Industry, any First Ladies, sporting a candy necklace, and that's why I love it: no Hollywood stars slinking around turning on the sex appeal, no dictators rousing the rabble, and no experts of any kind could get away, not that they would want to, with wearing a candy necklace. They are serious people, who deserve serious jewelry, but I—

You get my drift.

A fireman would love a candy necklace.

Not to wear—it might melt, sugar the skin, painful, I think— but to nibble and loll round the tongue after a hot day at the office.

I'd wear my candy necklace every day if I could. But then it would cease to be my candy necklace. It would become dull, rote, or worse than that: a tic, perhaps. You don't want to get typed when you're walking around a high school as *that weird teacher who wears the candy necklace.* I was a student once. I will burn in Hell, we all will, for what we did to that Spanish teacher who showed up one day sporting a bolo tie.

Maybe that explains how I got here.

Sorry, señor.

Whatever. Since I'm here, even more reason to choose to wear the candy necklace. I just have to choose the day carefully, that's all.

Like today, for instance.

For no other reason than it's May, and I've been refreshed by spring vacation, and summer suddenly seems more near than far, and I'm going to *win* something, this residency in Utah, or this artist's exchange I applied for, in Mexico, something's *bound* to happen, I mean, I can't just spend the rest of my life growing old with Cindy Fernandez, while she tells me, like the husband who flunked marriage counseling, how completely inadequate I am in every way, and in case for a second I happen to forget, she will have to—as a responsible person—remind me—*are you listening, Elizabeth? I think your mind was wandering when I told you for the ninety-fifth time how boring you are, and how crazy.*

No. This is not possible. This is a story I will tell one day and laugh. This is the tunnel before the light. My manuscript will be taken, and once I start winning, I will keep winning respect, travel, love, everything, I've got to, I must, because it is May, because the Tamale Lady cries *Tamales* these days with a little operatic trill in her voice, because of forsythia, because of some good song heard on the radio, because, although I broke a tooth the other day, at least I didn't break all of them: oh, I've got my reasons, isn't it reason enough that even though every afternoon after school I rush out for a quick infusion of *cafe con leche* and a square or two or three of guava paste, my pants, if I suck in my gut when I zip, still fit? Now that's a sign of divine favor if ever there was one, much better, more personal, than the sighting of the face of Jesus in a yucca plant or Mary in a dollop of whipped cream.

So, my children, we don the Candy Necklace.

*"Are you wearing a candy necklace?"*

So it begins. The mysterious charm of the candy necklace. Bob, in 9B, whose only ambition in life is to drive a bus, Bob, who wonders why the hell he has to go to school when bus driving is the life he's got in mind, and frankly, I wonder, too—why torture the both of us?—unclenches his fist and the punch he was about to bestow on Tim is forgotten. He's staring at my throat. "Is that a candy necklace?"

"Yup," I say, and he sits back, shocked: you can't wear a candy necklace as an adult without possessing a secret life, and how could a teacher *have* a secret life?

Role models don't have secret lives. That's how you know they are role models.

"Why are you wearing a candy necklace?" asks Samantha in 9C.

These are the beasts I am charming, my friends. I don't even have to learn the lyre. I just have to don my gay apparel with the right air—this is important—half indifference, half insouciance. Because this is Samantha, talking to me like a person. Samantha, who will use her voice from time to time to say, *I hate Elizabeth.* Far be it from me to suppress free speech, and this is my reward: Samantha is looking me over, she doesn't know what to think.

"My chocolate bar one's melted," I say, shrugging.

"Hahaha, very funny," she says sullenly, but she can't hide from me. She does think it's funny.

And so one day, all day, The Pax of the Candy Necklace reigns. It's still noisy, Cindy, Lucille, and Marcy are still insulting, Sammy's still groping, Elena is still improving her expertise at computer games, but no matter: for this day, anyway, the power shifts a little. They are not the only ones who are possessors of life. There's life in this corner, too, bub. A corpse does not wear a candy necklace.

Erica Reynolds is looking me over. It is not an unfriendly look, but then I never get an unfriendly look from Erica Reynolds. It is a *seeing* look; that's what it is, and she asks me, though she knows of course, the answer:

"Is that a candy necklace?"

"Uh-huh," I say, and she sits back, resplendent in her shining skin, and her shining hair, and the gold stars she has pasted to the outer corners of her eyes. Oh, I know what she's thinking, I know what they're *all* thinking, the thought leaps from head to head and they can't help themselves, they are powerless to resist, and I like it that way.

*Candy necklace,* they think, the girls resting their palms for a second at the base of the throat, *candy necklace, candy necklace, hmmm, hmmm, maybe I . . .*

*Hmmm.*

Martin looks up from his desk, which he is straightening, and sees the girls standing in his door.

He knows these girls by sight, but not by name; they are ninth-grade girls, and he teaches tenth grade and up.

"Yes?" he says.

"We're looking for somebody. Sarah Patel. Have you seen her?"

"I don't know her. What does she look like?"

"Long dark hair. Dark skin. *Very* dark skin." They begin to giggle.

"No. I haven't seen her around."

"Well, if you *do* see her"—more giggles—"tell her we're looking for her, okay?"

"That's the message? And who are you?"

"Oh, she knows who we are. She knows."

And with that, overcome with laughter, great gasps and gusts of it, they edge out of the doorway and run down the hall.

"Hey!" Martin shouts, watching them go. "Don't you want to tell me who you are?"

# the struggle of
# the books continues

Sometime in April, Naomi came up to me and said, "I hear you're looking for books."

"Yes!" I replied. "That would help. A lot."

"I'm the head of the Parents Book Committee. There's a warehouse where we get good deals. What do you want?"

I opened up the bright red Standards book and pointed to the high-school English page, congratulating myself as I did so for one act, anyway, of political acumen: these are the standards we're all supposed to reach toward. Who, from the schools chancellor on down, would give me an argument about them? "See this list?" I say. "These are the books suggested for high school. Any will do."

Not exactly. Some were way too challenging, and one or two I might have found hard to swallow, but on the whole it was a pretty good list. And there were over eighty to choose from, how could things go wrong?

Now, the beginning of May, Naomi comes up to me again, very excited. "We've got books!" she exclaims.

I run to the storeroom and open the boxes.

*A Tale of Two Cities,* abridged and rewritten for children.

*The Scarlet Pimpernel.*

*The Ancient Mariner and Other Poems.*

"These aren't on the list," I say.

"We got a great deal," she says, cheerfully.

"I bet you did."

Books, books, everywhere, but not a page to read. For if I walk into class and start talking about a dead albatross, I am dead meat.

And then I hear a rumor: *Martin's got a stash.* Locked away in the depths of his metal desk is one class set of *The Glass Menagerie.*

At the beginning, I would have lobbied for more: enough books so everyone could bring one home and read it. Now I am in Martin's room, staring in awe and relief at the books. They are pristine, like everything Martin touches. No rips, no ink, no drool, seemingly unread.

They won't look like this when they come back to him. *If* they come back to him. I know it. He knows it. And yet he hands them over.

Oh, noble man. Man of the cloth. Man of *two* cloths. The monk's robe. The flamenco sleeve.

"I met Tennessee Williams once," he says, confidingly. "I was very young."

Oh, *mysterious* man.


I live in a third-story walk-up in the improbable middle of midtown Manhattan, hidden away in a tenement somebody forgot to tear down and replace with a skyscraper. As a kid I used to dream of secret places, houses or shops nobody knew about but me, and this dream, anyway, has all but come true.

My apartment is a stage set.

The slant of the floor. The smell of cooking floating up the stairs. The street lamps sending harsh light into my windows at night. And most of all, the fire escape.

My apartment is a stage set for *The Glass Menagerie.*

Now I am lying in bed reading a book I haven't read since junior high. How heartbreaking it is. I had forgotten how much, or maybe I had to live a little bit longer to find out: the mother with her worn-out dreams of white Southern chivalry and her desperate *can-do* speeches, Laura with her withered leg and her craving for beauty, and Tom—our hero—the one who labors in the warehouse, but who dreams of escape, even if it's while he's standing on a fire escape instead of a balcony.

I've already blown *Romeo and Juliet.* Maybe I could have taught it if I had been the first teacher in the classroom. Or had had real time to prepare. Or had become so cavalier about failing—the way I feel now, for instance—that failing had no terrors for me. Whatever. Let Leon tell the parents that we're striding ahead, that I taught my students *Romeo and Juliet,* a genuine classic. I know I taught them nothing at all.

So why try again? Maybe because it's too hard not to try.

Meanwhile, the world of *The Glass Menagerie* has taken me over completely: the moon, the woozy sex and secret melancholy of the jazz bands on the radio, all those cigarettes, all that longing, the bricks and grime of a Midwestern city.

Oh so long ago. To me, it still seems so present. But is it?

Will they get it? A world before cell phones, computers, video games, the Internet, breast implants. Before TV even.

Yes, before TV.

My God. It seems like another century.

Oh, I forgot. It *is* another century.

*Golly.*

. . .

Monday morning.

"So, class," I start, "we're going to read *The Gla . . .*"

The roar begins. At least I can't accuse them of erratic behavior.

And as I try to get through to them, illustrating my affinity with that bad old, dirty old century by rolling my eyes and mouthing words like a kind of silent movie heroine—*if only I had subtitles!*—I think of the scene that I read the day before.

Tom stumbles in drunk, and tells Laura of the wonders he has seen out there, the moment in the movie theater when the light dims, and anything at all might happen, and the magic show afterward, when a magician, the Great Malvolio, in front of everyone, escapes from a nailed-shut coffin.

*You know it don't take much intelligence to get yourself into a nailed-up coffin, Laura, says Tom. But who in hell ever got himself out of one without removing one nail?*

Who indeed?

He takes me in his arms.

Not face-to-face; that would be too forward, for people who have been hardly introduced. No. He stands behind me and gently locks his arms around my shoulders, and rests his cheek against my hair.

The weight of a man's cheek against my hair. The bone speaking to bone.

How it begins.

The body, I mean. How it uncovers that thing that was there all along, like those keys you had been searching for, until they finally reappear on the hook you always hang them on.

And now his mouth is softly grazing down my neck.

There are few things better than kisses down the neck. It is what we need other people for. Try kissing your *own* neck, and see how far it gets you.

How it all starts up again. The body remembering its native folk dances. The tremor in the thighs, the blood doing do-si-dos and Virginia reels, the skin and the wet which need no music, and the tongue: the tongue suddenly speaking in tongues. How could it be, that we, the thighs, the blood, the skin, the wet, the throat, the mouth, the tongue, could have been removed from this so long?

How lonely we were.

They say it's like riding a bicycle.

That is, of course, when they're not saying that it tastes like chicken.

So. It's been a long time. It's been such a long time, and all the particles of my body are leaping around, crying out, *Me first! No, me! NO, ME!* and I don't know what to do, except to tell them to *be patient, we'll all get our turn,* and is it like riding a bicycle?

Well, yes, in a way, it is, though I guess it's an insult to think of him as a bicycle, when he is so obviously—the evidence, in case I ever had my doubts, is right here—a man.

*A man.*

*Jesus. Sometimes you forget those things exist.*

A man, then. A man I am riding like a bicycle.

I take him from the side of the house, and wrap my palms round his handlebars, and throw my leg over him, and we're off.

*Oh yes we are.*

Down the driveway, skidding on the gravel, swerving—*what a swerve*—as a dog—at least, I *think* it's a dog—nips at the back wheel.

And then we are flying.

Flying down one of those shade-dappled, sun-dappled avenues, sweating like maniacs, my bicycle and I, as I ring the bell for sheer exuberance: *ring,* goes the bell, *ring, ring,* it goes, *And look, Ma, no hands, No, no, whatever you do, don't look, Ma, hands,* and *ring,* goes the bell, *ring ring,* and *oh*

It is seven in the morning. I roll over to turn my alarm clock off.

Alex, my bicycle.

Yes, the music teacher at the School of the New Millennium.

In our waking lives, we have had only the blandest and most minimal of conversations. But in dreams, baby, in dreams . . .

"Yo, Miss, you a hot girl?" Randolph suddenly asks, in the middle of 9C.

Whatever can he mean?

I mean, I *think* I know what he means, but can I possibly be right? I am, after all, horrible thought, old enough to be his mother. And such are the complexities and swiftness of teen slang, *hot girl* could mean anything at all. It could mean *crack girl*. Or *fat girl*. Or *stupid girl*. Or *ugly girl*. Or *unbathed girl*. But no matter what he's asking, what am I supposed to say?

I don't want to flatter myself, that I am irresistible, when it is so obviously untrue, but something is going on. I can feel it. A little bubble of incandescence. Something is definitely in the air, some waft from my dream, perhaps, some stray hope involving Mexico, or Utah.

I happen to know hope is a very sexy thing.

The room quiets, waiting for my response.

"What I am," I say sternly, "is a hot-tempered girl."

Sammy Morales slumps in his chair and, spreading his thighs, looks me over.

"Uh-oh, Miss. If I was your boyfriend, I wouldn't like that."

*If you were my boyfriend, I'd shoot myself.*

Oh, Lordy. Now I know why spring comes but once a year. I mean, *look* at me: shabby clothes, bad moods, dark circles under my eyes from night after night of insomnia. Shouldn't they be asking someone else this question? Or is there so much erotic energy about that after it has electrified every youth in the room there's still a stray kilowatt or two that can come to me?

"Turn to page seventy-two," I quaver, in my best schoolmarm style, but they're not having it.

"I bet you're a hot girl, Miss. I can tell."

*snickersnickersnickersnicker.*

The sad thing is, Randolph has never been nicer to me. He's calling me Miss, he's soft and polite, and taking his lead, the class quiets down, waiting for my response.

"Seventy-two, as I said, seventy-two, please," I say, but no one takes these kinds of directions seriously anymore. Even Sarah, my friend. She's sitting in the front row, eyes sparkling at the distracting comedy of it all, waiting for what amusing thing will happen next.

The boys are looking at me. Could it be, have they finally figured out, that I am in possession of . . .

A bosom?

Yes, I think they have.

At this moment, comes a knock on the door. It is Nkruma, come to return a book.

Nkruma. He's so much cooler than me. If anyone knew what a hot girl is, it would, of course, be him.

"Listen," I whisper. "What is a hot girl? Some kind of special slang? Or does it mean what I think it means?"

He shakes his head and throws the boys a look of irritated disgust, a look I would patent if I could. "It means what you think it means."

And now it's my time to confess: I know it's completely inappropriate, which is why, of course, Randolph is doing it, but it tickles me, a little bit, even to be asked the question. At least, for a minute or two, we were having a conversation. At least people were paying attention, though it did seem to be more to my bosom than anything I said.

I mean, Bob, just the other day, called me a fucking lesbian and Sammy told me I was always in a bad mood because I had no friends. Isn't hot girl an improvement? Proof, perhaps, that as Leon once told me, I would slowly get through to the kids?

What does it mean, really, to be a hot girl?

Is it like chili? Or chicken vindaloo? A scald of spice on the lips and roof of the mouth, a gulp of ice water, and just when you think you're done with it, the heat doubles back and gets you again?

Well?

The answer to your question, Randolph, is yes. I suppose I am.

In the office, I see Alex, and before I can stop myself, a little voice in my brain starts whispering excitedly: *Ooh ooh ooh. Remember him?*

Sure I remember him. It's just that in the dream he was filled with kind attentions and tons of *savoir faire*—in the dream this lad could *kiss*—but in the office of the School of the New Millennium, he's hunched over a desk, face in his hands.

*Oh my God*, I think. *Is it possible? I think he's even more depressed about being here than I am.*

Lunchtime, and Amy Lee and I are sitting on the sofa out in the hall, having a girl talk.

What are we going to do with Amy Lee? So small, so pretty, so vulnerable, so completely without guile, so desperately hungry for loving approval I worry about her, for such hunger is dangerous in a girl so pretty and innocent: I'd like to build a wall around Amy Lee.

She is failing abysmally of course, but her attempts to improve her situation are so bereft of cunning I worry about her even more.

For instance: she writes a paper, or begins one, anyway, and in her childish handwriting describes how she knew she was failing, so she went to church and prayed she would pass.

"Only work will help you pass," I say to Amy, and she hangs her head sadly; not that she resents me for giving her the standard teacher lecture: she was just hoping against hope that prayer would work.

I have given my students an extra credit assignment, a way to make up for past mistakes: write a report about one aspect of the life of the thirties, the era of *The Glass Menagerie*.

Amy hands me a perfectly if impersonally written essay about Maurice Chevalier.

"Who is Maurice Chevalier?" I ask her casually.

"Who?" she says.

"You know, the guy you wrote the paper on?" I say. "You didn't write this paper. Where'd you get it?"

"The Internet," she answers. "But you know, I retyped every word!"

Oh, Amy, Amy, Amy, what are we going to do with her? Every time she throws her arms around me and cries, "Oh! I love you! I love you so much!" I cringe for her. Louis has told me how she has tried the same thing with him, but of course with him it is different. *I love you!* she cries, like an outtake from a French farce, and Louis, with a daughter of his own, and a consciousness of sexual harassment laws, runs from her embrace; but one day, Amy, there might be someone who will not.

And now I've got my chance to mold a young mind. There's something Amy needs to know.

"Elizabeth," she says. "How do you learn to kiss?"

"Why do you want to know?" I say.

"My boyfriend broke up with me. He told me I am no good at kissing."

I have met this boyfriend. He is in eleventh grade, a sullen, half-literate boy of no particular charm, and quite a few pimples, and if I had to make a guess, it would be that *he* might be no good at kissing, and furthermore—and this is what scares me—kissing is just a metaphor for something else. Something I can't imagine Amy is ready for, but could easily be pressured into.

"Forget him. He's not good enough for you. He really isn't."

She sighs. "He told me I was no good at kissing. So how do you learn, Elizabeth?"

I half laugh, ready to launch into the old Carnegie Hall joke— *Practice, practice, practice*—but Amy doesn't need jokes. She needs guidance.

"Are *you* good at kissing?" she says. "I bet you are."

I am suddenly very conscious of my lips. And then I decide, *What the hell. Why not. The truth.* "I've been told I'm not bad." I shrug. "Pretty good, actually." A strange realization, for when I was Amy's age, I was as innocent, as naive, as backward, as terrified, as you could get.

"Could you give me some tips?"

"Oh, Amy. It's not hard. It just kind of happens, that's all. It's kind of like writing a paper. The more you do it, the better you get at it. That's why we do multiple drafts."

She's looking at me with her big melting eyes.

"But you're *not* doing it, are you?" I say, grabbing at her hands. "Believe me, Amy, you are way too young to have a boyfriend. Look, I don't know how to say this, but I think you're just not ready. I think people can be really mean, there's no harm in waiting, Amy, and when you do, you will find out that you, too, are good at kissing."

"That's what my mom says. She says boys can be really bad."

I sigh.

I know Amy is fourteen years old, but sometimes she seems to me like she's ten. Eight.

Oh, what is going to happen to Amy Lee?


"Well?" says my friend Belle.

We are on the telephone, and I have just told her of the bicycle dream.

The bicycle dream, while, it is generally agreed, is a nice little dream, it is not as good as the George Clooney Dream.

But what could be? That was a masterpiece of subtle understatement: George and me, lying on a broken-down sofa, he in jeans, me in an old summer dress, both of us barefoot. My feet are resting in his lap, and he is stroking them.

The girls love the George Clooney dream. They love that feeling of drowsy summer. They love the crummy clothes on us, no need to dress up when sharing a private moment. But most of all, they love George stroking my feet.

Yes, the George Clooney Dream is the best. My friend Laura has asked me if she could rent it.

But the bicycle dream has a distinct advantage. Those kisses down the neck, they were good, they were *expert*. And Alex and I, we have, at least, been introduced.

So, "What about him?" says Belle.

I consider Alex. He's not ugly. He's not a bad guy. He's not an idiot. He's not unpleasant. I believe he's straight. It's just—that he's gloomy, that's all. Not that I blame him. I'm pretty gloomy myself these days. It must not be very attractive. Put the two of us together, and the heart cries out . . .

*George, George, give me George. I've washed my feet, I have.*

"It's like this," I say. "You know how in *The Diary of Anne Frank* they're all locked together in this annex and then she becomes a teenager, and *this* is the adolescence she is going to have, and she wants to fall in love, and there's only one boy in the vicinity: Peter Van Daam? It's him or no one. So I look at it this way. It's not like our situations are exactly similar. But. The School of the Dark Ages, at least in *this* situation, is my annex. And Alex—*he* is my Peter Van Daam."

Spring, and a young man's fancy turns to one thing: taking off his clothes.

In 9A, Maurice wakes from a gentle snooze and starts unbuttoning his shirt.

I give him the teacher look. *Oh please. Here?*

Maurice finishes unbuttoning and slides the shirt off.

I should be thankful for small favors, I suppose. He's wearing an undershirt.

The teacher look—the quiet glare, the irritated *You've got to be kidding* eyebrows—suggests: *Perhaps you want to put that back on.*

"Look at her!" he gasps, suddenly modest, wrapping his arms around his chest. "She's getting aroused!"

*Oh man.*

And in 9C, Randolph begins to take off his pants.

Okay, sweatpants. But how am I to know he's wearing a skinny little set of shorts underneath? All I know is, he's taking off his pants.

"Randolph," I say. "Is this what you want to be doing?"

"I'm *hot*."

The teacher look again. The oh-so-ineffectual glare as the pants slide down and down . . .

"Stop staring at my dick! She's staring at my dick!"

What a day this has been, what a day. It's almost like an epidemic, this boys' desire to display their parts. The temptation to say, *Your what? Your dick? Oh, so that's what it was,* is very strong.

But something, luckily, holds me back. It is the vision of the meeting I would have to endure in Leon's office.

"Randolph told me that you . . . *uh* . . . sexually harassed him."

"I was only making a joke."

"He said you were being sarcastic. Elizabeth, we have discussed sarcasm. Sarcasm doesn't help."

*It helps me.*

In the past few years, there's been a story in the news about a teacher who had a romance, had a baby, with a thirteen-year-old student of hers. An attractive woman in her thirties. Hauled up on statutory rape charges, she stood there in court, announcing how the two of them loved each other, and then she was sent off to jail, only to resume the romance when she was freed to have *another* baby with this boy. How old was he then? Getting on, all of fifteen, perhaps, and now, considering the boys before me, the mind whirls.

What was that first date like?

*She: Nice here, isn't it?*

*He: S'okay.*

*She: I think I'm just going to have a Diet Coke. I'm not hungry. But what about you? I'll get you anything you want. Fries, Big Mac, shake. Go on, splurge. It's on me.*

*He: Okay.*

*She: So, what'll it be?*

*He: You know. What you said. Fries. Big Mac. Shake. Coke. Double fries.*

*She gets the food. They eat and drink in silence.*

*She: I think we need to talk.*

*He: Did you fart?*

*She: Oh, of course not.*

*He: I think you farted.*

*She: Honey, it's not me. Listen . . .*

*He: Well, somebody farted.*

*She: Well, maybe somebody did. But that's not that important, is it? Not when there's . . . us.*

*He: It is rank in here. It reeks.*

*She: What difference does it make if it's rank or not? As long as we're together, baby.*

*He: You've got a booger hanging out of your nose. Let me pull it off. It's a big one. (He reaches out his hand. She clasps it tightly.)*

*She: Now I've got you. Big beautiful hands you've got. Manly hands.*

*He: Can I have some more fries?*

*She: Sometimes in class, I sit there and think of your hands. Your big, sensitive hands.*

*He: Can I have some more fries?*

*She: They say age matters. For me, it doesn't matter at all. You, for instance, are really mature for your age. There are thirty-five-year-olds less mature than you. Believe me.*

*He: Can I have some more fries?*

*She: Maybe the world will judge us. It doesn't matter. They just judge what they don't understand. Or what they're jealous of! Listen, baby. It doesn't matter what the world says. Let them nurse their little prejudices, if it makes them feel better. But you and I . . . two hearts . . . two souls . . . We were meant to be together. I've been waiting for you all my life. Sex, it's a natural thing, it's a beautiful thing. It's never wrong when two people love each other.*

*He: Are you looking at my dick? Are you getting aroused?*

*She: Umm . . .*

*He: Can I have some more fries?*

Sarah Patel puts her key into her new front door.

She sighs.

Nobody's home. Nobody will be home for hours. She will do her homework, the little of it she's got, saving the hated math for last, and then unpack a few boxes with the radio on.

It's all too much. The new apartment, the new school, the strange looks Helen shoots her in the hall—as if she's going to have a fit or something—and that feeling she has—*is she paranoid?*—that she's being watched. That people are laughing at her.

Who would want to watch her? She is nobody. And why would they laugh? She's not funny.

"I need a break," says Sarah Patel, standing in her front hall.

She has checked a book out of the library. One of those mysteries with a little bit of romance thrown in? The kind she can't stop reading, once she starts? She'll do her homework. She'll unpack a couple of boxes. Then she'll make herself a cup of hot chocolate—oh, she could do that. She skipped lunch!—and lie on her bed and drink that chocolate, and read that book.

Now there's a plan.

Sarah rifles through the mail she has taken out of the mailbox, smiling a little as she thinks about it.

Bills, she sees. A letter from Our Senator. A letter for her mom, from an auntie Sarah has never met, back in India. And a letter—for her.

Who would be sending her a letter?

Sarah weighs the envelope in her hand. It has no return address, and her name and address are made out in impersonal block letters, in a handwriting she can't recognize.

She rips it open.

YOU STUPID FAT UGLY BITCH, she reads. SOON YOU'RE GOING TO DIE.

Through the halls the two of them walk: American daughters of Pakistani parents. Mona with her glasses, Nadia with her head scarf. Good girls. Modest girls. Obedient girls. Hardworking girls. *Grinds.* How minimal are the assignments that come their way. They try to expand on them, add that extra paragraph, grab for every extra bonus point, but still, it's not enough. It frustrates them. They can't learn anything. They can't show people what they know, they can't strut their stuff.

Here, in the Land of The Hall, no one is interested in their stuff.

Strange being a grind. Reading the words, writing the equations, slipping into their loose innocuous clothes and arriving *here,* where other girls are shouting and practicing dance routines and banging open lockers where the grinds can glimpse, sneakily, though nobody cares and nobody's watching, the message pasted inside: *I WANT TO HAVE SEX. I WANT TO HAVE SEX. I WANT TO HAVE SEXSEXSEXSEXSEX.*

They cannot imagine those words coming out of their lips, never mind pasting them in their locker.

Are they pretty? Are they not pretty? This is not something to worry about, they are told. They are pretty enough. Their eyes are dark. Their skin is like wheat. They are good girls, obedient girls. Things will come in their own time, when they are supposed to come.

Now—they must concentrate.

Do their homework. Read the *Times*. Study for their exams. Get into Harvard, or Yale, or Princeton, or Columbia.

And after? Nadia and Mona have talked about this. Nadia would like to go and *do* something. Work for the U.N., maybe? Help the women in Afghanistan? Strive to make a difference?

And Mona? Well, she's not sure. "I just want to get a great GPA," she says. "Then we'll see."

Now that's a plan. You need a plan. Otherwise, you drift off, you have a baby at sixteen, you start saying those words you will say all your life: *You want fries with that?*

This fate is not for the grinds.

So they walk through the halls, no prettier or uglier than the other girls shouting: *HE SAID AND THEN I SAID AND THEN HE SAID AND THEN I . . .*

Let them shout. They will not always be shouting. Not so joyously, anyway.

Yes, it is true. They know it is true. This will all be forgotten when the grinds grind their way to the future that is theirs.

*Keep your eye on the star.*

Easy, when you are invisible.

But they don't mind being invisible. Why should they? What would they like people to see?

*HE SAID AND I SAID AND HE SAID AND I SAID . . .*

This is a test, they know, this is a test, and they are so good at tests. When they pass this test, as they have passed, and will pass, all others, they will leave this behind.

*If only the years weren't so long.*

"You will see how short they are," Nadia's father laughs, but even though she respects and loves him, this she cannot believe: *endless*, these years.

They must concentrate, concentrate; nothing must get in their way.


Erica Reynolds and Eric Antonelli. Eric Antonelli and Erica Reynolds. Sometime this year, they began to drift together, and now, if you see one, somewhere in the vicinity is the other. Who can explain it? The strange synchronicity of these two? Both slight; both pale; light brown hair, dark blue eyes: they look more like brother and sister than most brothers and sisters. And here they are, clowning through the halls, as one.

Are they boyfriend and girlfriend? I don't think so. Erica has announced that she doesn't want a boyfriend yet; she is, after all, only fourteen years old; she has a plan, other things to do and be. I believe her. And besides, these two, walking chastely side by side in the hall: this is not sex I'm looking at. This is something far rarer. There are no girl's magazines suggesting lip gloss or midriff tops for this one. This is not that kind of maneuvering, this is not a boy or girl you can get or not get. This is—if you believe in this kind of thing, and let's say for the purpose of this argument, we do: *destiny*.

They are comrades.

Do they see it? How similar they look? How even their names, chosen by separate parents in separate bedrooms, locked like to like?

Am I jealous?

You bet I am. It gets lonely out here in the world.

Anyway, what I feel is of no concern. Pondering my feelings, and only my own feelings, that's what adolescents are supposed to do. I have entered the Age of Generosity. And so I watch them. Those two.

If they have a leader, she's it. She's a bold girl, confident and capable at every task. She's finessed the social structure of high school, slipping from one clique to another with ease.

As for Eric . . .

I identify with him. I don't know if he knows this. This is certainly not something I should tell *him*. *Hey. You're moody, you don't always do the easy thing, the thing that is good for you? Cool! You're like me! You want a role model? Choose me!*

No, let Eric get his own role models, if that's what he's hunting for. Though could it be that without even craning his neck a little, he's found one?

Erica breaks her middle finger, and comes to school with a splint keeping it stiff. She enjoys waving her hand around, giving everyone a *Hey—I can't help it—fuck you*. I think it's funny. It would be too tempting *not* to try it. Erica's deportment is perfect: her expression poker-face bland, as her gestures suddenly go mad and melodramatic: *Fuck you—oops, didn't mean that—fuck you—sorry—fuck you, and—as I was saying—fuck you.*

A slight, knowing smile crosses both Erica's and Eric's lips.

And then Costume Day comes—one of those events invented to keep the children amused. Kids are wandering around the hall wearing masks and snippets of this and that: I *think* they're costumes, but I can't be sure.

Erica comes to class in a version of her usual garb: loose blue T-shirt, jeans, eye glitter, blue nail polish, that finger neatly splinted and taped.

Eric comes to class in loose blue T-shirt, jeans, eye glitter, blue nail polish, middle finger neatly splinted and taped.

And so they are together. Waving their hands, eager to offer the answer to every question.

*Any question! Ask us anything!*

*Fuck you and fuck you . . . and oops, sorry, didn't mean it—this splint you know—Fuck you.*

Their expressions are mild and guileless. Looks they must have practiced at home: they are too good to be unrehearsed. Solemn and helpful as butlers, they wave and wave. Erica doesn't crack a smile. But sometimes suppressed laughter—at least I think it's laughter—ripples across Eric Antonelli's face.


Arden, the good boy.

The light-skinned black kid with the old man's face.

No gossip, no jokes, no punches for Arden.

No schoolwork, either. He does not possess the remarkable talent of someone like Ken, who could work on a battlefield, if that's what he had to do.

Arden sits, and as class begins, he takes out his pencil, and like those characters in fairy tales, who must stay silent for years while they complete some elaborate yet seemingly pointless task, he starts to draw mythical beasts: eighty-four minutes of pencil drawings, each feather, scale, talon, painstakingly crosshatched. It is as good a way as any to while away the time.

Silvia, the bad girl.

Not that I know she's a bad girl: just that she has that aura; the aura of girls on the subway who make up for their height and build with a cold challenging glare that you would be a fool to meet. Let her best you with that glance, because she would cut you in a minute; and furthermore, you, as far as this girl goes, would deserve to be cut.

What a beautiful girl is Silvia. The long black hair, the pure white oval face, those dark eyes: a Renaissance virgin with a tough-girl swagger. The boys must love our Silvia.

These two rescue me.

It seems like a strong word, rescue. But these two, simply by allowing me to feel a little useful, without in any way feeling humiliated, or unlike myself, keep me going.


"Why do you sit here and do nothing?"

9A is over. Most of the students have picked up their stuff and left. And as Arden slips his sketches into his notebook, I find myself suddenly asking him this question.

He looks startled. "I don't know," he says.

"It would be so easy for you to do a little something. Even if you're not interested, to go through the motions, to do enough to pass. But if you do nothing—I have no choice but to fail you."

"Yeah, I know. But what's the point of trying? I can't hear, I can't think, it's been like this all year. I can't take it. I have a headache all the time. So I just . . . gave up, that's all."

I find myself beginning to smile. "You know," I say, "high school is not the world."

I pull up a chair and look hard into his face. " I see what's going on here," I tell him. "How certain kids make it impossible for everyone else. They talk louder, and they talk meaner, and I can't seem to do anything about it. But just because they think they're top of the heap now, they are in for a very mean surprise, Arden. The day's going to come, they're going to graduate, and they're going to find out in a hurry that they are not so great. That nobody cares that they were popular in high school."

Arden looks shocked. "Really?"

So this is what it's like to be young: you remember things, and now that I am back in high school, I am remembering a lot, but this is what is hard to remember: what it is like not to know what later you will find out.

"Yes. Really."

"You mean, it doesn't matter if you're popular in high school?"

"In the long run? Not very much."

"But *why?*"

"That's a hard question. What I'll say is, things that sometimes seem so important now end up not being important at all."

"That's not fair." But he's smiling as he thinks about it, he can't seem to help himself; and I'm smiling, too. Let us not mince words: the thought of some of my students getting their comeuppance makes me very very happy.

"Oh, it's fair all right," I say, leaning in conspiratorially. Arden, beaming, leans in right back.


Silvia wants to pass this class, she tells me. It's not the first time I've heard this kind of thing. Kids come up, you say okay, offer equal partnership, and that's not really what they were looking for: they were hoping you'd do everything for them, that goodwill on their part would be enough, and when it is not, back into class they fade.

Silvia has done this before as well. But now it's May, and, "I'm serious, Elizabeth. Is it too late?"

"No, not too late. What do you want to do about it?"

"It's my writing. I need help. Do you have any free time?"

"I tutor once a week after school. Could you come?"

"I work every afternoon after school. Weekends, too. How about lunch?"

My heart sinks. "Lunch?"

"Yeah."

"Okay," I say, though at first I don't want to.

When 9A is over, the rest of the kids file out, and here's Silvia, waiting.

"I'm going to give you a writing exercise," I tell her. "While you're doing that, I'm going to run down and get a cup of soup. That okay? You want anything?"

"Sure it's okay. A banana nut muffin." She gives me some change.

"I'll be back in a minute. I'll lock the door when I go out. Don't let anybody in, all right? I don't think I'm supposed to leave you alone in here. But we won't tell anybody, will we?"

"No," says Silvia, smiling.

Is it that easy to win over tough-girl Silvia?

It seems to be.

·  ·  ·

Arden has begun to do his schoolwork.

It's not easy, he's neglected it for so long. But he's trying, and while usually the self-esteem dogma sticks in my throat, somehow, when it comes to Arden, I can't praise him enough. It's the sight of that young old man's face drinking it in that draws me on.

It's one of those days when the ball gets rolling the moment class begins and before I know it, a line of tap-dancing Rockettes could throw hand grenades in here and no one would even notice. In other words, a typical day.

Arden, Ken, and a few other kids are huddled around me while I read a story out loud. It's ridiculous to do this, I know. They are certainly old enough—or should be—to read it to themselves. But one of my students is so dyslexic he is incapable of that. Besides, it's too noisy for even the best student to concentrate. When I read out loud, I can put the expression in, and create a little bit of space where thinking can happen.

Arden is happy. He loves the lesson. He loves thinking about the story. He loves worrying about little nuggets of vocabulary.

"Why?" he'll ask, about a character's motive, or a word. "Why, Elizabeth?" and I'll tell him, and each time he gets something, he grins.

"Pretty interesting, don't you think?" I say.

He nods.

And then, as class is almost over, I hear a voice from a great distance:

"Hey!" shouts Erica. "What's going on over there?"

"We're discussing a story."

"Why don't you discuss it with us?"

"I tried, Erica. But I'm not going to shout. You want to discuss the story, come over here and join us. The water's fine."

But Erica can't come.

Oh, she wants to. She likes literature. Moreover, she likes me. But Erica, despite her good work habits and her friendliness, has managed to be popular.

Popular has rules. Like, *Don't come over to the other side of the class. Don't ally yourself with those who are not as cool as you. Don't cooperate, even if you want to.*

I know that Erica does. Poor Erica.

So Arden is a bit of a nerd. So is Ken. I am, I guess, too.

Today we're pretty smug about it. For nerds have no rules. To be a nerd—a true nerd, that is—is a kind of anarchy.

*Viva la Nerdisma!*

We're so out we can do whatever we goddamn please.


After writing for a while Silvia puts down her pen.

"I got good news, today, Elizabeth," she says.

I'm sitting on a desk, spooning soup into my mouth.

"What?" I say.

"I'm not pregnant. It's been hard to concentrate, you know, thinking I was pregnant?"

"I bet. How old are you, Silvia?"

"Fifteen."

"Be more careful next time, will you?" I say.

"I will."

And this is how our odd little relationship begins.

Silvia stays after class, I give her something to do then lock her in, I run down and get lunch for the both of us, she shows me what she's done and I critique it. She's a smart girl, a quick learner, and in the strange silence of Room 313 she's beginning to get things she's never gotten before. "Wow," she'll say, "I never knew I could write that much." "That's what happens when it's quiet," I reply, "and you can think, and you try a little. Interesting, isn't it?"

And she nods, and Silvia and I drift into talking about Life. Or she starts telling me about her life, because next to her I have had no life at all.

It's a funny thing about Silvia. I don't really like my students calling me by my first name. We are not the same, after all, there is a gap between us. But Silvia is a *woman*. She really is. In her fifteen years, she has experienced more than I ever will; first-name basis is the only thing that makes sense.

Silvia, in her calm voice, tells me of her troubled family, and of herself: how she once was even in a knife fight with a girl, *cutting her just a little, she deserved it, Elizabeth,* and of being picked up by the cops, and how scared she was, how truly scared, and how she wanted everything to be different, but she was still proud of what she was.

The things Silvia tells me are so far out of my experience I have nothing to add. I was sheltered, I was taken care of, I never felt in danger, I never felt I had to pull a knife on anyone. I can't judge her, not that I care to. It doesn't seem to matter what she tells me: I like Silvia. I see goodness in her. I like the way she treats me, as neither her superior nor her inferior, but as a comrade, girls together in the world.

The tranquillity in Room 313 is seductive. I look up and Annie, from 9C, is pressing her face to the glass. She's a sweet girl, easily led, and since 9C is in chaos, that is where she goes. But she could just as easily go the other way.

"Can I come in and do my work? It looks so quiet in there."

"Sure. But we're not going to let in any of the boys, are we?"

No. We're not.

Sometimes Sarah joins us.

Me and the girls. Writing. Eating. Gossiping. This is the life.

But today, Silvia and I are alone. She looks down at the composition she's just finished and smiles at her progress. She's pleased, can't believe it, really, and now it's time to relax a little. Silvia, unpeeling the paper from her muffin, is ready to talk.

About men. Her men.

Her love life is complicated, and not surprisingly, busy. She went out with that one, and she doesn't want to talk about him, she had to get rid of him, he was so mean, but now she has a sweet one: actually, she has two.

"What about you, Elizabeth?" she says. "Your men. What about yours?"

I laugh, and throw the remains of my lunch into the wastebasket. "I don't have any men."

"You don't? But you must. You've got to have a man in your life."

"You're telling me." I lean back in my chair and put my legs up on my desk in a gesture of defiant annoyance.

Silvia begins to laugh. "Actually, you don't need *a* man. You need two. At least two. You've got to keep it a secret from them, but that's not hard. Let's face it: They're not very bright."

## between classes

Sarah can see the envelope, taped onto her locker, halfway down the hall.

She closes her eyes. She knows what it is. She's been expecting it. Still, each time, each day, it's a shock.

Each day she thinks, *I should tell.*

Each day she doesn't.

*Who would she tell?*

She's a big girl. She can take care of this herself.

She creeps up to her locker.

Imagine being afraid of your locker.

Sarah opens the envelope.

*YOU STUPID UGLY BITCH. TODAY IS THE LAST DAY OF YOUR LIFE.*

## how i learned to
## speak honestly to black people

Like a lot of Americans, I have lived a pretty segregated life.

I didn't set out to do that. It just . . . kind of happened. By the decisions I made or didn't make. By the way groups, for so many reasons, pull themselves apart.

It's not that I didn't know black people, or see them. Walk out my door and here we are: every shade of skin, permutation of hair, and fold of eyelid. We're all here, all of us, and it's exhilarating: what I miss most about New York whenever I leave. Who would have it any other way?

But, this is public space I'm talking about. In public, we *are* all in this together. Privately . . . it gets more complicated.

Now, here at the School of the New Millennium, I find myself thinking about race. Not that I want to. I would be perfectly happy to just make an aesthetic note to myself that everyone here is a different color, and then move on. However, whether I want to think about it or not, race—or rather, our perceptions of what our race makes us, and how other races treat us—is part of the picture.

Still, when I try to understand what race might actually mean, and how it plays itself out inside the psyches of different groups, I get confused. Scared, even. How honest should I be? Am I ready to uncover ugly truths about myself?

Part of me is sick of the whole thing. I know, a luxury, a white luxury, but I'm being honest here, right? When I mention the book *Black Boy*, by Richard Wright, and Marcy shrieks, "That's racist!" I know this is not racial sensitivity I'm dealing with; this is just one more teenager exercising her crossing-all-ethnic-boundaries-God-given right to be a jerk. And when I talk to Marcy's mother on the phone, and I hear her hostility, and distrust of me, her utter dismissal of my request that her daughter simply behave, am I right to hear this under text, what I think she's really saying: *white bitch?* or for some other mothers: *Jewish bitch?* And if I am, what am I supposed to do with this information, implied but unspoken? Apologize? For what?

But then I have to ask myself if it is my own fear and inadequacy, my reluctance to own up to buried prejudices, that makes me find them in others instead. To this, I have no answer.

A good part of me knows that race is a construct, something we hammer out so the world has a shape; there can't be us if there is no them. Race is mutable. And if you don't believe me, open up the paper and read the long litany of tribal battles: Hutu versus Tutsi; Serb versus Croat; Turk versus Kurd. From your safe distance, do you see a difference between them?

What does it mean to be black? It's not the same to be from Barbados or Brooklyn or Atlanta or Senegal, any more than it is the same to be from Germany or the Appalachians or Bialystok. How much does a doctor from Dakar have in common with an aspiring hip-hop star from Watts? How much do I have in common with a white evangelist from Iowa?

It's not that race doesn't matter. I have all around me the evidence that in so many subtle and not so subtle ways, it does. It's just that other things matter, too. Like class, for instance. It seems to me that many of the problems that we Americans *say* are about race are actually about class. That class division, as opposed to racial division, is really our dirty secret.

That bad things happen to people because of their race I have no doubt. And furthermore, that shared experience, and the memory of that experience, binds you to people that otherwise you might not have much to say to at all. But when some of my black students say what *black* is—and believe me, they do—it says less about what black really is than what they think they are. And what they think they are confuses me. It troubles me, and I don't know what to make of it.

Take the strange case of Samantha, in 9C. She is a good-looking girl with a head of beaded braids and a wide malicious smile; a girl who's always eager to stick her head in the door and yell how much she hates me. I find I don't have the energy to hate her back, because her attempts at character assassination go no further than that. Besides, I have begun to see this shout as a kind of ritual greeting, akin to the Cantonese asking each other, first thing, "Have you eaten yet?"

Samantha has a secret. She is very smart. Not that she spends most of her time acting smart; she spends most of it acting hostile. But I see it in her face, a quick perceptive gleam that enters her eyes sometimes. And once she writes a paper, a good, eloquent one, and when I praise it, before she can stop herself, she beams. She tries to hide the pleasure my praise gives her, but too late: once I get a glimpse of the truth I know the whole story.

Rachel has seen it, too. Tried to pep talk her. Surely it must be deeply boring to go around acting dumb when brainy is what you are.

"What do you want me to do?" Samantha said to her. "Be white?"

"White?" sputtered Rachel. "Look in my face, missy, and then, please tell me, how white I am?"

Now why Samantha has decided that to act like the person she essentially is—intelligent—is to act white, I cannot even attempt to say. I don't know Samantha well enough for that. It would all come out as a stupid generalization. All I know is, this is something that the black teachers at the School of the New Millennium talk about a lot. If I hear little bits of it, I know I am simply privileged to eavesdrop on a family discussion. I listen, I never say anything, for I know that what makes me merely unhappy makes them deeply miserable.

"Nigger," Shawn shouts to Randolph. "Get off me, nigger. Leave me alone."

"No, nigger! No!" Randolph responds.

"I'm going to *get* you!"

"Ha ha, you try, nigger! You try!"

Of all the words bellowed in my classroom I hate this one the most. As far as offensive goes, it leaves *Homo* in the dust, and then some. I know that it's common street talk, but that doesn't mean I have to like it.

Yet how can I, as a white person, announce that I find this word racially offensive? That it hurts my ears the way the word JAP does, because the subtext is that you are one kind of person, and one only? That you are embracing the ugliest things the world thinks of you? That you are in love with your own slavery, because it makes you feel at home?

I'm not saying I don't understand it. I think I do. I'm just saying I don't like it.

Do we see the irony in this?

We do.

"Please don't use that word," I snap.

It works. That simple outburst, no explanation, no attempt to talk about Southern sheriffs and the back of the bus: here are directions pure and simple. Anyone can follow them. And they do.

Shawn looks up. He's got a little cat face, and big dreamy eyes, like a silent film star.

"I've been saying that word all my life," he says.

"Maybe so. But not here."

Shawn contemplates this. It makes sense to him. He can be as offensive as he likes, just not here.

And just as I'm opening my mouth to tell the students what pages of *The Glass Menagerie* we should pretend to read, I hear another voice.

A soft, insidious, rather creepy voice.

*"Have you heard of the Middle Passage?"*

It's Randolph, ventriloquizing again.

I won't say the boy isn't gifted: he is. Simply by folding his hands in front of him and letting a look of *faux* concern cross his face—I don't know how he does it—he becomes the parody of every adult who takes things way too seriously.

"You know the lady with the dreads?" he says, slipping out of character.

Oh God. Carla.

I don't know Carla very well. She teaches in the elementary school. I just have an impression: the dreads, the dangling silver earrings, the soft, slow, humane voice. A woman with a mission.

A woman who told me once, after a meeting, that maybe—just maybe—I didn't love the children enough.

Maybe she's right.

Carla. Part of me wants to be like that. Smiling. Concerned. Perhaps a bit . . . humorless? No matter. Carla has that aura of teachery goodness that I, I know, do not. And we need people like her, maybe a lot more than we need people like me. Or so I am supposed to think.

The boys, black and white, start to giggle.

"That's what she says to me, when I say nigger," Randolph continues. "I say nigger, and this is what she does: 'Have you ever heard of the Middle Passage? Do you know what happened during the Middle Passage? Do you know what happened to our people? Do you know about the suffering of our . . . People?'"

The boys are really laughing now. They laugh and laugh and laugh.

Another typical day in 9B. Noise, chaos, bad feeling, Peter Garcia in his corner, trying to read his copy of *The Hobbit*. Elena jumps up.

"Look at us," she says, cheerfully. "We're all black and Spanish."

Which we're not. But Elena sees what she wants to see.

"Black and Spanish people," she says, "are . . . *everywhere!*"

"In music!" she announces.

She starts walking around the room. "Look at music, and

what do you see? A black person. A Spanish person. You see any white people? No. You see black people! Spanish people! Yes! We're everywhere. In music. And . . ."

She stops for a second, pondering.

"And, and, and . . . ," she says,

". . . jail. Yes!" she says happily, having decided what it was she wanted to say. "We're everywhere! Music—and jail!"

Elena is not a student I usually give much thought to. She sits on Cindy's side of the room and follows the leader. But now I'm trying to understand. Is she joking? It's a good joke, a bitter joke, if she is. Maybe I'm wrong, but I don't think so. Irony is not Elena's forte.

And that's when it happens. I had tried earlier that year to challenge certain assumptions. Maybe I had tried not very well. Maybe I was—oh, hell, I *was*—out of my depth. But that's what those articles I had brought to class in response to the Amadou Diallo case were about. My version of the lecture on the Middle Passage.

I couldn't do it then. I wasn't prepared.

But now it doesn't seem to matter anymore if I'm prepared or not. For I'm suddenly angry for the children who have to hear this and maybe half believe it, and the other children who don't believe it, but have to pay the consequences because some people do. Anger these days has gotten a bad rap, but it has its purposes. Sometimes it is the only thing that frees you to speak the truth.

I hate the word *nigger*. I don't care that people think it's fun. I know at the core of it is self-loathing.

I pull Stephen Thomas into the hall, and I give him a speech, and then when I'm done I do the same thing to Charles. I don't care that I'm a white lady and they are black kids. That I should be careful, and sensitive, and delicate.

This is what I say:

"Did you hear what she said?" I ask. "Did you? Why do you let her say things like that? How come no one challenges her, how come no one gets insulted? *I* don't think that's all you're capable of. I think you're smart. So why do you listen to her? Why do you let her get away with it? If *I* said that, you'd say I was a racist! And you'd be right! So don't you understand when she says that, she's a racist, too? And someone should tell her to just shut up!"

I glare at Stephen and wait for his response.

And it comes: the smile that lets me know he never was my enemy, the witty arc of the brow.

"You're right," he says.

"Well, do better. It's not for people like her to decide what you can do."

I glare at Charles.

He's tilted his face to one side, mulling my speech over, very serious.

"You're right," he says.

"So?" I say. "What are you going to do about it?"

"And furthermore . . ."

"Yes?"

"She's not even Spanish. She's . . . Dominican."

The men are laughing.

"CAT FIGHT!" they shout. "YOU GO, GIRL! GIVE IT TO HER! OH, YES! THAT'S A GOOD ONE! GIVE IT TO HER! WHATSCHEDO? STEAL YOUR MAN?"

Sarah Patel cannot believe what is happening to her. She just cannot believe it.

A hand tangles in her hair and pulls her head back, hard.

She is too shocked to yell. Too shocked to say, *Help me. Please. Help me.*

Why does she have to yell, anyway? Why don't they know?

She's not praying. It's what she *had* been doing. She had been praying hard. Every Sunday, she went with her family to church and prayed for the letters to stop. But now she's forgotten about prayer.

This is all that counts. This is all there ever was. Everything else was something she had imagined. A silly dream.

This is what is real. This day in spring so warm and soft and flowery, and the men laughing, and her heart going so fast it's as if *it* wants to beat her, too.

*Oh.*

She is flailing.

She doesn't know how to do this, but her body is doing it for her. Her hands fly up, they scratch, they grab, she doesn't know what they're doing, just something, *anything*, to make it stop.

"YEAH!" the men yell. "FIGHT BACK! YOU CAN DO IT!"

*Help me. Help me.*

"Cute, aren't they?" one man says to the other.

"I like the dark one. The dark one is *hot*."

Sarah feels something explode inside her face.

## the most beautiful girl
## in the ninth grade

Girls keep disappearing on me, but not the ones I expect.

First, Sarah Patel. I look toward her usual seat in 9C and her benign face is not there. I feel a little let down, and write it off as the flu.

Then, Helen. One day Maria, the aide, comes to see me and says, "I'm here to pick up Helen's assignments for the next two weeks. She's not going to be coming to school for a while."

Helen is not a person who's made a big impression on me. She is a pretty enough, quiet enough, cooperative enough girl; pleasant and no trouble. "Helen? Whatschedo?"

Maria shakes her head. "You don't want to know."

Then Nadia. No ardent serious glance. No modest self-containment in the midst of chaos. I miss her.

Then Mona. She knocks on my door at the end of 9A.

"Elizabeth? I'm not supposed to be here. But could you give me the work for the next two weeks?"

"You're not supposed to be here? Why not?"

A shocked stricken look comes across her face. "I did a bad thing. I did a very bad thing."

"You?" I say. "I can't believe that. You could never do a bad thing, not in my eyes."

Mona turns away. When I find out what she's done, I change my mind.

．．．

After Helen chased her through the streets, after Sarah thought she had lost her in the crowd, after she mounted the steps to the number-seven train and looked around, and thought she was safe, after Helen pushed her way into Sarah's subway car, and began screaming again, after Zuleika turned off her Walkman and with her impersonal instinct for justice awake once more, looked at Sarah, whom she hardly knew, and said, "Run to another car. I'll take care of it," after Zuleika, with nothing but the power of a Popular Girl, ordered Helen to stop, after Sarah, in another car, clung trembling to a subway pole, after Zuleika got off at her stop, and Helen and Sarah, in their separate cars, rode to their destination, after Sarah got off the train and glanced around and there was no one, after she began to walk briskly, but not running, she didn't want anyone to know she was afraid, after Helen was right behind her, taunting her, after Sarah *did* begin to run, after she felt the tug in her hair, after a group of men gathered round and couldn't stop laughing, taking bets on one or the other, the dark one, the fair one, after Helen punched Sarah in the face, and broke her nose, after all that, Helen was dragged into Leon's office and Leon and June and Tom surrounded her and the interrogation began.

   "Why did you do it?"
   "I don't know."
   "Why did you do it?"
   "I don't know."
   "Why did you do it?"
   "I don't know."

"*Why* did you do it?"

"Because I *felt* like it!"

"And what about the letters?"

"What letters?"

"*These* letters."

The letters Sarah had shown no one, but had carefully hoarded, were spread out on the table.

"Oh. Those."

For one moment Helen looked both terrified and relieved.

"I didn't write those letters. Mona and Nadia wrote those letters."


"Why did you do it?"

"I don't know," said Nadia.

"Why did you do it?"

"I don't *know*," she said.

Tom was looking at her.

Although she had wanted, from time to time, for people to look at her, really look, to admire the papers she handed in, and exclaim on her intelligence, her hard work, her neat margins; and she had wanted other things, too, other things that even while sitting here—*the principal's office, how could this be, the principal's office*—she could not admit to herself, yes, even though she had wanted, more than anything, to shine, and have others blink in her light, she finally understood the advantage of that costume that so frightened her, since she couldn't help but take it personally: the burqua. Yes, that was exactly what she wanted to be wearing right now. A cloth cage her Afghani sisters had been forced into wearing, yards of fabric covering the body from head to foot with a circle of thin mesh to breathe through and another mesh across the eyes. So this is what it felt like to be visible. A nightmare. Give her the burqua then, not yards but miles of darkness into which she could sink.

"Why did you do it, Nadia? It's so unlike you. Why did you do it?"

Because it was fun.

This was something she couldn't say, and she knew it.

"You can talk to me. I'm Tom. You can tell me everything."

Because it was fun.

And it *had* been fun, hadn't it, though it was hard to remember it exactly, a thin mesh was already floating in front of her eyes, so it was hard to see it the way it was, before she found out it had never been a joke to Helen. It wasn't what she meant, that's what she wanted to say, she didn't know Sarah was going to get her nose broken. But it had been fun, all of it. Starting with the miracle of Helen befriending them. Her family was Irani, but had come so long ago that Helen had no foreignness in her. She was an American girl, the complete deal, plucked brows, shiny nails, lips agleam with lip gloss. It was a feat, this act of transformation, something that took years.

And now Helen had run out of things to groom. She was bored. She was sick of dorky Sarah hanging around. "'Helen, do you have the math homework? I don't understand the math homework.' The way she whines. The way she never leaves you alone."

Then those late afternoons in Mona's bedroom, after their

homework was done, writing the letters, giggling like mad, each trying to top the other's insults, because they were competitive girls, in everything, it was fun. It's not that she would do it again—not the way she was feeling now—but it had been a thrill to write those letters, to have a secret, to walk through the halls and look in Sarah's dark and damaged face.

"You know," said Tom, "poor Sarah had to have her nose reset. Pray the reset takes, Nadia. Pray she doesn't need an operation."

"Would my parents have to pay?"

"We'll see," said Tom, folding his arms.

Through the glass door, Nadia heard a commotion. Mona's mother and father.

"Two weeks. Suspended for two weeks? *Mona?*"

"Yes," said June. "Be glad she's not expelled."

"Two weeks." said Mona's mother. "The year's almost done! What is this going to do to her GPA?"


It is this question, perhaps, the one about Mona's GPA, that makes Tom tell us all what happened. Before that, nobody's telling. Judy and June are caught up in the everyday running of the school; Maria, lips pressed tight, patrols the halls; and Leon is off at some meeting or other trying to convince somebody to give us our charter status, so that—well, I don't know exactly why it's so important to him. That's another thing nobody's saying. All I know is, Tom comes into the cafeteria, where the high-school teachers are sitting around, collating report cards, and he starts raving: which is not the way I rave, it's a mere glimmer of a *I'm throwing myself off this balcony, I really am, I promise, let me sing one more aria, and oh, one more after that,* this is controlled raving, but, because Tom does it, it's very effective. Tom is disgusted, and all I know is, I wouldn't want him disgusted with me.

"Why are we doing this?" he cries, surveying the report cards we are alphabetizing and neatly stacking. "Why bother? Half the school's failing. Most of the rest—barely passing! And our A students? They're—suspended!"

He tells us the story of Sarah Patel, and we all leap into our assigned roles. Now it's Rachel who's raving, demanding *justice, justice, for Sarah Patel, she should sue, if someone did that to her child, Rachel wouldn't rest, that brute would be dead, dead, expelled at least, isn't that the least we can do, aren't we going to do something,* and Miriam, in her calm way, says, "Why?" and Vivian, in *her* calm way, answers, "They were jealous. Because she is so pretty, that's what I think," and Martin is shaking his head at the dark mystery of girls: how the blood welling up and trickling out of their bodies every month has made them bloodthirsty in a way that boys are not, and I am thinking of Sarah Patel.

My first little friend. Well, not really a friend. An adult can't be friends with a fourteen-year-old. It's why being in the classroom is so lonely. But with her unabashed curiosity and openheartedness, she was my first friendly presence. Why her? I think. I have a list of people you could torture. Hey, I would help. But why Sarah?

And Tom is explaining why, and he's right, of course. He's talking about Nadia and Mona, the good girls, so uncool they could walk through the halls unafraid, they were that invisible, that far beneath anybody's radar, and how they acted like it didn't bother them, but it must have, because when Helen began cooking up the plot, they were ready, eager, to come up with their own baroque refinements, not just one letter, but many, and Sarah— was perfect, a girl who always walked through the halls alone, a girl who wouldn't fight back, but for once, even as I'm listening, I'm pondering not the words but the physical answer to the question. I'm running through my mind once more the first time Sarah came up to me, to confess a little secret, and I was struck— I couldn't help myself—by her beauty, and the serious innocence in her face.

"I'm praying for a miracle," says Sarah Patel.

I am sitting in the office, the phone at my ear. "Maybe you won't need a miracle. It sounds like things will probably be okay."

"I don't want to have an operation. So I'm praying. To Jesus. He's going to take care of it, I know it. My mother is going to church on Sunday, and she's going to pray for me, and everybody's going to pray for me, and will you pray for me, Elizabeth? Will you do that?"

"Yes, Sarah," I say. "I'll pray for you."

"The days are kinda long," she says. "Everybody's out of the house, and I rest, and I watch TV, and do you know there are preachers on TV? Some of those programs are pretty good. You'd be amazed at how good they are. And I read the Bible. When you're feeling bad, nothing helps like the Bible. No matter where you open it, it's like it's really talking to you."

Why does this confession shock me? More than, say, if Sarah had admitted that she was experimenting with Kahlúa (*It's so good, Elizabeth! Mix it with milk and you can drink the whole bottle!*)

or cigarettes or marijuana or meeting older men in their taxicabs (*And then he touched me, and do you think a thirty-year age difference is too much?*).

It shocks me, or rather, confuses me, because, I suppose, I am a sinner. Because, forgive me, I can imagine myself in Nadia's and Mona's place, laughing while writing those terrible letters, but I can't see myself, on the couch, reading the Bible, watching the preacher shows on TV, and not for laughs, but for comfort.

"Do you read the Bible, Elizabeth? You should, you know. No matter what your problem, there's always an answer there."

But before I can think of an honest yet kind reply, I hear her take a breath.

"Why'd she do it, Elizabeth?"

"I don't know."

"I mean, we were *friends*. Her mother and my mother are friends, so I guess that's always the kind of friends we were, but we were friends. And then we stopped being friends, okay. But she didn't have to break my nose. The blood was everywhere. *Everywhere*. I still can't believe it."

"Sarah, how can I explain this, when I don't understand it myself? People do mean things. They do really mean things. To people who don't deserve it. And that's the important thing. Whatever happened has nothing to do with you. It was only about her, something ugly in her. Not you. You have to know that."

"And what about Mona and Nadia?" she says. "I don't even know those girls. So why'd they do it? How could they hate me, when they don't even know me?"

.  .  .

When I thank Zuleika for helping Sarah on the train, the befuddled irritated look I have seen before crosses her face. I want to laugh with pleasure at the richness of Zuleika's secret: the angel locked in her, the one who gets out when she's not watching, but I don't. As Tom pointed out, she was the only one in the whole business who acted well, and so I give her a little room.

She shrugs, sullenly, and I settle back to wait for the girls.

And they come, all on the same day.

Helen brazening it out and Mona and Nadia sliding down in their seats, and Sarah, walking tentatively, as if her legs had been screwed out of her hip sockets and then screwed in again, and she was trying them out for the first time.

Is it just my imagination, or does the crowd in the hall part for her a little? Is she no longer quite the invisible girl? Has she acquired, just a little bit, an aura of victimy glamor?

"You look the same," I tell her. "Just the same. The most beautiful girl in the ninth grade."

"Oh no, Elizabeth, I think I have a little bump . . ."

"Don't be silly. You don't."

"I prayed," says Sarah. "I prayed."


I am taking my favorite religious fanatic out to lunch. It is the least I can do. "So, Sarah," I say. "Where do you want to go?"

"I don't know. I'm not hungry. I just don't want to see them. Every time I see them, it makes me sick."

"Well, then, have I got the place for you."

How excited I am to introduce Sarah into the Temple of the Teacher's Coffee Shop. Those orange vinyl booths. Those wagon wheel chandeliers. Those swollen cakes on pedestals, beneath domes of Plexiglas. *Here we are, Sarah,* I want to say. *We've taken our time machine, back to the last decades of the twentieth century. Any second now one of those waitresses—see the one by the rice pudding?— is going to call you Hon.*

But of course she doesn't. The waitress is old and poky and sullen. I can't blame her. It mustn't be that much fun, years and years of toting trays around, growing older and pokier, not that you're alone in this: your clientele is tottering right behind you, and sometimes ahead.

The junior, planted in her usual booth, looks up from her cup of tea and her Diet Plate, gives a friendly wave, and goes back to perusing the Princeton catalogue.

Sarah sniffs at the air, notes the absence, no doubt, of the usual local scents: no oil, no garlic, no tomato sauce, no onions, no chickens sizzling on the grills.

"What *is* this place?" she whispers.

"It's where the teachers go to hide," I reply. "Isn't it great? No students ever come here. Except for her, and we let her. So come on, let's take a seat at the counter. I love the counter, don't you? And order anything you want, Sarah. It's on me."

Not much of an offer, I suppose, in one of the worst restaurants for miles.

"I don't want anything," Sarah says primly, staring at one of the pastries: a huge baton threaded with chocolate and cinnamon and powdered with sugar.

"What about that?"

"Oh, I couldn't. I'm too fat."

"Come on. If you're too fat, my pinkie is obese."

"Really, Elizabeth. I really am."

"Sarah, don't turn anorexic on me, okay? I tell you what. We'll split it. How's that for a solution? You see, when we figure out something together as a family . . ."

Sarah smiles, sadly. If she has a flaw, it is this: she has not much of a bent for parody. It means I sometimes run out of things to say to her.

No matter. We are served. Her Diet Coke, my coffee, the Pastry Thing. I break it apart, and give each of us a half, and "This looks *so* good," I say, and stick in my fork and lift a morsel to my mouth.

It is stale, of course. Very stale, and even when fresh, I would imagine, it had been tasteless, as if the time machine allows us glimpses and sounds but no flavors: that would be too much. I could send it back, as if it were a fine bottle of wine at a fine restaurant, but then I would have to admit that it isn't very good, that this is one more lesson in a lifetime of promise and disappointment.

Sarah saws away with her knife and fork, taking tiny bites, and so do I, two well-bred girls of different generations, but none of this, I see, is distracting her, or giving her pleasure. Maybe even a gooey hot fudge sundae wouldn't do it.

She puts down her silverware. "You know I want to transfer," she says. "I want to get out of here. But my mother says no matter where I go there are going to be mean people who want to do mean things and there's no point in running away. She says I've got to face it. She says I'll get over it. But Elizabeth . . . I'm *not* getting over it."

"It's too new, Sarah. You will, you know. Your mother's right."

"But I just can't stand it. Helen broke my nose, and *I* had to go to the doctor, and *I* was the one who was hurt, and *I* was the one who was scared, and what happened? She's pulled out of school for two weeks! You know what that means? I had to stay home for two weeks. The day I come back, she comes back! It's like we did the same thing, but we didn't, did we? Is that fair?"

Sarah stares ahead. "Jesus tells me to forgive. He tells me to love the sinner. And it's bad, but I can't forgive. I look at Helen, and you know, she still gives me these weird smiles? As if she's not sorry at all. As if she's waiting for me, and wants me to know it. As if she's planning to hurt me some more."

"Helen's not going to hurt you," I say. "Don't worry. She knows if she did that, she'd get in real trouble. I think you're safe."

"But *I* want to hurt her."

"Of course you do."

"Jesus tells me to forgive. So why can't I do it?"

"Sarah, I am a girl who keeps a grudge. I'm great at grudges. I really am. So I have an idea: maybe what you should do is go on with things, and let *me* not forgive her. What do you think?"

"I'm afraid to go home," she says. "Afraid to walk through the streets by myself. I'm fifteen years old, and my mother's picking me up at school. The problem is, she works till five. And it takes her maybe half an hour to get over here. So I need someone to wait with until my mother gets to school. Would you wait with me?"

Now I am the one who does a bad thing.

I get off work at 3:40. By the time the day is done, *I'm* done. All I can think of is leaving.

"Five-thirty?" I say. "I can't."

A look crosses her face.

"I mean," I say, "I have an appointment. Can't do it. Not tonight. How about . . ."

She doesn't believe me. I can tell. Maybe if I were wearing a burqua, but it's all in my face, all of it, my lie and my panic at the lie, and my desire to simply run away.

"How about Thursday?" I try to backtrack. "I tutor on Thursday? And other Mondays! I'm sure I can do it, just not this one."

"It's okay," she says.

But it's not. And at that moment, quite simply, Sarah unhooks herself.

First she chose me, then she *unchooses* me. Maybe, for the first time, she sees what I'm really like.

I'm nothing much. Or at least, when Sarah looks at me in the coffee shop, I feel like nothing much.

So off she goes, Sarah Patel, and it's not that we still don't talk, or that I don't see her Thursdays, or that I don't try to make amends, and offer to stay after school with her when, after all, I can't think of anything I would want to do less, but she doesn't take those offers. She just doesn't like me the way she used to. I can tell.

And maybe that's okay. Maybe her friendliness to adults masked her loneliness among her peers. Maybe in another year or two Sarah will be slinking around in midriff tops and beating off boys with sticks.

Or she will be that quiet junior, in the coffee shop, making plans.

Whatever she does, she won't need more mothers, or in my case, I think, big sisters to help her through.

But as far as right now goes, she's not doing very well. She's not coming to school that much. I suppose her mother is, after all, indulging her. When Sarah does come to school, some of the kids try to be friendly, but she does not respond.

She starts wearing a large wooden cross around her neck. The first time I see it, I can't believe it. It's so graphic, this cross, no delicate talisman of silver or gold but a true crucifix, dangling from a leather thong. Such extravagant display. It is so unlike her.

But who is she, after all?

In class—when she comes to class, that is—Sarah reads. But no longer those girl-books she used to enjoy, those amalgams of romance and mystery that I would sometimes see her reading under the table: *she couldn't help herself, she just had to know what happened next.*

Now she sits at her desk, a huge Bible open before her, moving her lips while she reads, though she never moved her lips while reading before.

She is praying.

*Sarah,* I want to say. *Put the book down. Be brave. Have fun. You are, after all, the most beautiful girl in the ninth grade. Don't hide. It's no use. They'll find you anyway, until they stop looking, and that's even worse. Confound them, go ahead, shine. There are people to love and a time machine to take, into the future.*

I say nothing of the sort. I say nothing at all, except trivialities, to Sarah Patel.

Adam Patel walks through the halls of the school, alone.

For most of the year, he sat in the back of 9A, clowning with Maurice. But now Maurice has basically stopped coming to class. So in 9A, too, Adam is alone.

He doesn't look lonely, though. He wears, instead, the air of being here, but not here, a pleased distracted look, as if he had just thought of something incredibly interesting, and was turning it around in his mind and considering it from every angle, and he probably is.

Through all the chaos of this semester, Adam has kept working. Not, as he would insist, because he cares about grades; leave that kind of worry to the grinds, those who need blue ribbons and applause to keep them going. No, Adam works simply because his brain has got to gnaw on something.

We have supposedly read *The Glass Menagerie*. Poor Tom. Poor Laura. Poor Amanda. Poor—yes, even he—poor Gentleman Caller. Having killed off Romeo and Juliet long before their time we have proceeded to smash *The Glass Menagerie* to smithereens.

Now 9A is taking a writing exam about it. Most of my students ignore the word "test." They just continue chatting. But not Adam, and twenty minutes before class is over, he puts down his pen and hands his composition in to me.

*Should Tom go? Should he stay?* That was one of the questions I asked, and these were the first sentences of his reply:

*Of course Tom has to go. Though it might be hard for Laura, if he stays and gives up his dreams he will become a bitter bitter man.*

Later I will see the flaws in this paper; the grammar mistakes, places that might have been more developed. But gazing down at Adam Patel's bold flowing handwriting, what I see is thought, moving along and inventing itself as it made its way down the page.

And may I remind you, he has done this in a room where they are currently reenacting the San Francisco Earthquake.

"Adam," I say. "This is great."

What a look on that face. What a mystified, amazed look, as if he were staring at something nobody else could see, but he could see it very clearly.

"I don't know what happened," he says. "I started writing, and it was like the ideas took over. They just kept coming, one after the other. I didn't even know I thought them. I could have gone on for hours."

I feel tears spring into my eyes.

Am I really crying because a boy wrote a paper?

"Well, you did it," I say. "You really really did. Sometimes it's like that, when it's right."

Adam smiles. That little-smart-boy smile.

But when he goes back to his seat, he looks stunned. I ignore the usual screaming, laughing, and chair banging around him and go up to his chair and squat beside it.

"So, Adam," I say, "what do you think you're going to be?"

"I don't know yet. I'm thinking of a few things."

"Well, you could be anything."

"I know."

"You could be a writer," I say. "You really could. But don't be a poet. Then you'd have to end up doing something like teach high-school English."

Adam laughs.

Oh, I like that laugh, that quiet-smart-boy laugh; the laugh of someone enjoying a secret handshake with the world.

I'm looking out for Adam Patel. Yes I am. I don't care that I'm supposed to love them all equally. With Adam, I don't need some Balkan folk dance to break down barriers. This is a boy I can trust. This is a boy who isn't going to run to Leon and tell him I'm damaging his self-esteem.

I must admit, I play to his corner of the room a little bit. And I *am* playing. It is almost June, after all. My expectations have sunk so low I have no expectations. It is a very Zen place to be. An emptiness, in which I can start jitterbugging around the room, crying out, *Come on, Vincent, how about a dance, just one dance,* or yelling out, when the din gets to be too much, *Heard melodies are sweet, but those unheard are sweeter,* and when the din grows greater than that, what better moment for a few lines from that old Dylan song, *Any day now, any way now, I will be released,* and when the din grows louder still, *yes,* even louder, what else will do but . . .

*prayer?*

I fall to my knees. I lift up mine arms and raise mine eyes to the ceiling: "My God," I exclaim, "what have I done to deserve this?"

9A just screams harder.

Funny, I thought that somehow this would subdue them.

But Adam?

In his corner, he laughs. Not too loud, as if, almost, to himself.

Adam Patel, on my suggestion, hies himself over to the Forty-second Street Library to work on a research project. He sidles up to me in class and whispers, conspiratorially, "I went to the library."

"Cool, isn't it?" I say.

"Yeah."

"Ever been there before?"

"No."

"That place has history. Those lions. Those murals. Big world out there," I say, "on the other end of the number-seven line."

"I know," sighs Adam Patel.

It's a neat stunt he's pulled off. I don't know how he's done it. For they respect him, his fellow students. They listen when he speaks, at least the ones who can listen to anybody. Kids are friendly to him, and he is friendly in turn, but somehow, it is agreed: Adam Patel is *of* them, but *not* of them. What goes on around here is of interest to him, but it doesn't define him. Adam Patel is his own man.

Not that some people don't try to change the situation.

We are doing one more writing assignment, or trying to, when Kimberly and Rosalie park themselves on either side of him.

Of these two girls, what can I say? One is white, short, stocky, and blond; the other black, short, and stocky. As the months have gone on, they have delighted in showing me in as many ways as possible that they despise me. So relentless and so dull is their mission that it makes me almost like Cindy Fernandez.

Yes, I know Cindy is impossible, and she's made my life a misery. But something in me admires the stupid opera of her attempts to bring me and others like me down.

All her self-dramatizing speeches. Her ripped-up papers, her threats to call the *New York Times*. Never mind the way some of the male teachers have told me she has tried to trap them into acts of sexual harassment. Squeezing her enormous breasts while sitting in Louis's class. Sidling up to Calvin and talking to him in a little-girl voice about her period.

It just shows how essentially young, and dumb, and self-destructive she is, for what man, especially Calvin, who is so private, wants to discuss a woman's period? She thinks she's being sexy, and they . . .

*Oh, Cindy.*

But these two girls are different. Not for them eternal life in the ninth grade. They know how to look out for themselves. They please who they have to please, and as for those they deem powerless . . .

*And now they've got Adam.*

What in the world could they say to Adam Patel?

"I *love* your hair," says one, twining one of Adam's curls around her finger.

Adam doesn't say quit it, and he doesn't smile either. Adam ignores her. He keeps writing.

"It's so silky," cries the other, sticking her hand in. "Can you believe this amazing hair?"

"Could I have your hair? I *want* this hair."

And Adam?

How does he do it? He keeps writing.

*Look at them,* I think. *Picking and plucking like . . . like . . . monkeys.*

*Oh, Elizabeth. What a thought.*

It shocks even me, though that is exactly what they look like.

*Are you jealous?* I ask myself.

*Do you want to be the one playing with Adam's hair?*

*Well?*

And while I think these dangerous thoughts, and the girls, inflamed by Adam's indifference, play more flagrantly, he keeps writing.

They're a striking trio, these three. The white girl. The black girl. And Adam, with his fine, almost Nordic features, and his black black skin, the teeniest of smirks on his face.

*How strange. The whole idea of classification.*

Look at Adam. Those bones of his? They're Caucasian, more classically Caucasian, than Kimberly's.

And he's blacker, far blacker, than Rosalie.

Yet he's not white. He's not black. He's . . .

Other.

Yes, that's what he is. Other. He's more *them* than *they* are.

Adam lives in a bad neighborhood. Drugs are sold in the vacant lots, and at night, a curious boy like Adam has to stay in, because of the guns going off.

Adam is of this neighborhood. He knows things I cannot even imagine knowing. But he is also *not* of this neighborhood. Because he reads, and he knows that this is not the only place there is. And to know that is to change everything.

I wonder if he gets lonely, being other?

No matter. Other is the only thing to be.


I am walking through the halls, as Vincent goes past me, trailing his McDonald's rubber T-Rex puppet behind him on a string.

Vincent has named him Geraldo.

"Sit, Geraldo. Heel, Geraldo. Roll over and play dead, Geraldo."

Geraldo sits, heels, and plays dead like he means it.

"Good *boy!*"

Unlike most of my students, who think they're funny, Vincent actually *is* funny. I stand and watch him, and as I'm watching, Adam comes running round the corner.

"I've got Geraldo!" he yells, snatching the string out of Vincent's hand.

"Hey! Give him back!"

No dice. Adam, that skinny thing, is running, Geraldo bouncing on his string, Vincent right behind them: "Geraldo! Geraldo! Come back to Papa!"

Yes, I know. Shouldn't I be saying, *Now, now, boys, no running in the hall?*

It is almost June. Those days, if they ever were, are over. Let them run.

How fast Adam is. And how good, it turns out, at maneuvering around all those obstacles of human flesh that get in his way. Vincent seems thick and bumbling in comparison, though that's partly Vincent's doing: he exaggerates his ineptitude the way Adam does his ease.

*I hope they make it. Wherever they think they're going. I hope they do.*

*Don't be morbid, Elizabeth. They will.*

They are, after all, the Leaders of Tomorrow, the three of them, especially the one in the middle, the one with the reptile's face.

*Oh come now.*

And if they don't, or make it partway, so what? They will be like most of us, and lucky to get that far.

Still.

I am thinking of Adam Patel, boy explorer. Dreaming of his Amazon, only an Amazon better and deeper and richer in rivers and birdsong than any Amazon ever entered before.

*Good luck, Adam.*

Let it be that Amazon that he will discover, and not something else.

You'd think somehow that talent, and heart, and brains would be enough, more than enough, to bring that boy wherever he wants to go. But it's not necessarily true. Things happen. You get sick. Or people you love get sick. The economy crumbles, or war comes, or a war gets fought inside you, you don't even know how or what for. All you know is, there's a skirmish, and there's a battle, and then there's another, and you don't even know what's happening, only that it's happening in you.

*This is not something we will speak of, Adam Patel.*

How can we speak of it? Adam doesn't have time for this kind of melancholy conversation. Adam Patel is running with a monster at his heels.

Only this monster is on a string. This monster, despite his ferocious appearance, is hollow inside. This monster is named . . . Geraldo.

Well. Maybe I will name my own monsters Geraldo. Maybe that's the way to defang them.

june
**the longest first five minutes**

## departures

Tom is doing the Smug Dance.

He's tucked his hands into the front pockets of his jeans and is waltzing around the Xerox room, an *I Love Everybody, Especially Myself* smile on his face.

Tom is leaving.

Yes, in two weeks, before the term is up, Tom will be leaving the School of the New Millennium. He wouldn't do this just for *anything*, but this is special. He had applied to a very exclusive program out at Stanford to train people who want to be principals, and he got in. He's starting right away.

"Oh, I'll be back," he says, still dancing. "Don't worry, you won't see the last of me."

Sure. Let's see what happens when those orange groves and California girls get ahold of him. You mark my words, the School of the Dark Ages will soon seem to him not only like a dream, but a dream dreamed by somebody else.

Somebody named, say, Elizabeth.

I didn't win the Writers at Work competition. I didn't win anything, though a few times, I came close. *This was a finalist, we loved it, very original. Try again next year.*

What if you can't even imagine a next year?

I, too, had applied to a program in Stanford, it turns out, for writers.

They didn't exactly laugh in my face. I was too insignificant to be laughed at, and I wrote it off, but now to see Tom dancing—

Well, I tell myself, more people want to be writers than principals, my competition was very very stiff, though sadly enough, we probably need good principals a lot more than we need good writers.

Anyway, it wasn't that rejection that hurt. It's the ones that come close that kill you.

That fellowship in Mexico? First runner-up.

This one merited a phone call. This one seemed to demand that the director, out of misguided kindness, had to tell me:

"If there were another place, you would have gotten it. They didn't reject you because of talent, Elizabeth. They *loved* your work. They rejected you because of something else."

"What?" I said.

"Oh, I can't say. Reasons. You just weren't what they were looking for," she said, brightly. "Try again next year."

So you see, by the time I called up the people in Utah to find out what I already suspected—that I hadn't won, but should try again next year—I was pretty wound up.

"You'll be sorry!" I raved on the phone. "You'll be sorry! They'll *all* be sorry!"

"I'm sure we will," the woman on the other end said primly, and hung up.

And here's Tom, dancing about, smoothly, easily, not breaking a sweat, not that he has to.

I wonder what it feels like, to have a future?

. . .

Well, it's happened. Our charter application has been accepted. Come September, we will officially be a charter school. What this means I'm not quite sure. All term I knew these machinations were going on, but I never paid that much attention. I had other things on my mind.

It turns out I'm not the only one. Leon is beaming, he's ecstatic, but among the teachers, now that it's too late to do anything about it, rumors are flying fast and furious:

*We'll lose our tenure.*

*And our benefits!*

*And our seniority!*

*It's a plot, a plot, so we can lose our tenure!*

Louis is glum.

"I told you, I told you, I *told* you to be careful. But did you listen? You just signed that agreement. You didn't have to. You'll see, running a school, handling all that money, I know the Board of Ed doesn't do a very good job, but soon they'll find out: it's a lot harder than they think."

Emergency meeting!

Calvin, our union representative, hands out the Conversion Charter School Agreement and tries to calm people down.

We will not lose our seniority.

We will not lose our benefits, either.

Any Board employee who works in a converted charter school will be on unlimited leave. If the school closes, or the employee decides to leave it, she may return to her former geographic district depending on her seniority.

But what does it mean, to go charter? And why do some people want it so much?

It's complicated. As far as I can see, it means that the school is no longer under the aegis of the Board of Ed. It's now run by a Parents Committee. The Board of Ed will give us a financial allotment, and will check up on us periodically, going over test scores and what have you, but the running of the school is up to us.

"The Board of Ed offers a very thorough course in financial management, and I took it," a parent is saying brightly.

Louis is shaking his head. "I used to run a business," he sighs. "Money management, it's hard. The Board of Ed may be inefficient, but because it's so big, it gets lots of discounts on books, materials, everything. And now? Look, I don't want to be pessimistic, but, most of these schools go under. Because of graft. Because people who have never handled large sums of money before suddenly end up handling them. It's too tempting. It goes to their heads. Or even if it's not graft, it's just a hard thing to do. Balancing all these different needs—Well. We'll give it a try. Maybe it'll work."


Judy is leaving.

She and I, we are very different people, and since the day I huddled in her office, snuffling over my guava pastry, we have spoken little, but for that time, I owe her—I know I do—eternal gratitude.

And now she's leaving.

And she's not the only one. The roaming army of Board of Ed Employees—special ed consultants, psychologists, social workers—are leaving, too. They are employees of the Board of Ed, and we are no longer under the umbrella of the Board of Ed.

"Don't tell anybody. I'm leaving, Elizabeth," says Judy. "When this school goes charter, I don't want to be here."

"Why? How does this affect you?"

She sighs. "We all know the Board of Ed is far from perfect. But at least, whatever decisions it makes, they're not personal. Now, everything is going to be. I couldn't last, trying to please everybody and trying to please Leon, too. No thanks. I mean, let's take just one example: that little matter of standards that everyone is talking about. What if you're on the Parents Committee, and it's *your* kid who's not up to the standards? You're going to let him fail? Or are you going to look for someone to blame? You think this school is stressful now?" she says. "Just wait."


Nkruma is leaving.

Nkruma, the role model to us role models, is leaving.

How could *Nkruma* be leaving?

Does a king just depose himself and leave his subjects?

How could Nkruma go like that, just leave us like that?

*Men.*

But when I think of some of the things I've heard him say, it begins to make sense.

That scene in the Teachers' Room. His outburst on Teacher Development Day. His advice to me to be a Fascist. Or to invent projects for those who are interested, ignoring the rest. Or the time he once said to me, "Trouble with you is, you care too much. I used to care. Not anymore."

This is a man who was seriously burning out. And unlike a lot of us, he wasn't going to drag himself through his days, giving less and less of the self he had less and less of to give, but to do something else.

I am walking through the streets one lunch period, thinking of Tom and Nkruma. How kind they've been to me. Rescuing me again and again when it all got to be too much, with never a word of criticism or complaint. I never knew how to thank them. Most of the time, I was too embarrassed to let those words pass my lips.

And now, who should I run into but Nkruma himself.

"So what are you going to do now?" I ask.

"I'm starting graduate school in social work in the fall."

"Social work? Nice to know you're taking the easy way out."

He laughs. "Ninety percent of what I do is social work anyway."

"Well, good luck."

"Thanks, I'll need it. I'm not sure I'm going to last."

"Of course you will."

"I don't know. I don't do too well in school. I like to talk back. I get kicked out of classes. You see, I've got this little problem," he says, half embarrassed, half proud, "with authority."

Somebody has broken the sink.

You know that sink that stands in the back of Room 313? I always wondered why it was there. But now I understand: it was there so it could get broken.

How could someone break a sink?

But there it is: not a chip to be wished away with white nail polish, but a huge chunk. Half a side of the sink has been broken off and spirited away.

I know not how, nor where it went. All I know is, one day I look toward that corner, and . . . *am I seeing things?*

"Wow!" says Peter Garcia. "Look what happened to the sink!"

I shut my eyes.

They never found the computer vandals. I suspected, somehow, they wouldn't. They pulled lunch cards and strutted around for a while and tried to wheedle kids into confessing, but nobody said a word, and so, eventually, the matter was dropped.

And now the sink.

And that's not all: somebody has scrawled some bit of Arabic-looking graffiti on the floor in dark red Magic Marker.

Why me? Why Room 313?

I mean, I don't see these things happen. I don't, I really don't, look up from my book and say cheerfully, "If you're going to swing a sledgehammer in here, dear, make sure you don't hit anybody."

No. These incidents simply happen, the way the boils in Egypt, all those centuries ago, must have happened: One day you're an innocent Egyptian, minding your own business, utterly boilless, and the next day: *boom*. Boils. Boils all over.

I'm not telling Leon.

I'm *not* telling Leon.

I'm almost out of here and I do not want to have this discussion about the sink.

Of course, the custodian could tell him, but I don't think he will. The custodian is miffed at me. A little while ago, he asked me out on a date, and I don't want to go into it, but he's just not for me. Rather than thinking of some clever way to let him down, I just froze stupidly. Result? He doesn't go into my room and do much cleaning anymore. So he hasn't seen the sink, or the graffiti.

Could the custodian have broken the sink?

*Now, Elizabeth, you are getting paranoid.*


The day has come, the day we've been waiting for, and people are excited.

Remember that book, *The Best Public Middle Schools in New York*? Which is how I found out about the School of the New Millennium in the first place? Now the writer is back. She's doing a new book, *The Best Public High Schools in New York*. We're all to be on our best behavior.

"Whatever happens, we have to keep her out of 313," I say to Martin, miserably.

"Don't be silly," he sniggers. "She's going to come into my

room, and see part of the lesson, but after that I'm going to escort her personally into Room 313 so she can see some *real* teaching being done."

"And you call yourself a Man of God," I sigh. "I wonder if it's too late to take the kids on an impromptu field trip."

How quiet the school is today. The children file in orderly crowds to class. Were there sedatives in the lemon wax that the custodian buffed into the floors? Or in the cakes laid out liberally in the office? Or are there some hypnotic powers woven into the fabric of Leon's new suit?

What spell are these kids under? Whatever it is, out in the hall, anyway, it's working. But in 9C, things continue as normal.

Is this the day someone says she's going to beat the fucking shit out of me, or is that another day? What does it matter? Kids will be kids, and man, I love 'em, and if only the writer of *The Best Public Middle Schools* would drop into Room 313 for a minute I would tell her how much I love 'em.

I look up, through the glass, and there they are. Leon. Tom. The writer. Strolling right past my classroom. How happy they all look. Chatting, and smiling, and nodding in agreement.

I wonder what they're saying. I wonder what people talk about when they chat, and smile, and nod in agreement.

*One of the best public high schools in New York.*

*What a joke.*

*Unless . . .* I shudder *. . . it's true.*

Maybe this is how it's done. Maybe deep in the bowels of Stuyvesant and Bronx High School of Science and Midwood there is one classroom, *one,* where all the evil and chaos and vandalized computers and broken sinks are concentrated so everybody else can be clean-spirited and free. Didn't I tell my classes—or try, anyway—that "The Lottery" is an allegory, and an allegory represents something found in life? Who's to say that we are not the sacrifice so that the harvest can come in, and the School of the New Millennium can be chosen as one of the best public high schools in New York?

What is the secret meaning of that graffiti on the floor?

Is there any way, any way at all to elude our fate?

It's all I can do not to rap on the glass.

*Come back! Watch me chat! Watch me smile! Watch me nod in agreement!*

I watch as they walk into Martin's class and shut the door.

That day, as I'm punching out, Leon walks up to me.

"Elizabeth, there's something I've got to talk to you about."

"Yes?"

"I hear that somebody's broken the sink. Is that true?"

"Yeah. I was meaning to tell you. I just kept forgetting."

"And someone has drawn graffiti all over the floor. That true, too?"

"Yes, Leon, that's true, too."

"In dark red ink."

"Yes, that's the color."

He sighs. "Did you see who did it?"

"No, Leon, I wasn't there. Don't you think if they were doing it when I was around, I would have tried to stop them?"

He shakes his head. I can tell, he wants to believe me, he is not a malicious man, but . . . "The custodian's upset about it."

"I don't blame him. I'm sorry."

"Damaging school property like that," says Leon. "It's bad. It's very very bad."

And one morning, almost at the end of the term, Zuleika comes up to me.

"Listen, Elizabeth," she says. "I was watching TV last night, and I saw this program about these reporters who were investigating Death Row cases . . . and . . . is *that* what you were trying to teach us?"

"Yeah," I say, "it was. I thought it was a way to talk about Amadou Diallo *without* talking about Amadou Diallo. . . . Oh, never mind. It doesn't matter now."

I know I should respond more graciously. It would be the right thing to do. So I add a few words: "Interesting, isn't it? Those reporters, doing all that work, changing that governor's mind like that."

"Yeah."

Leon would call this a triumph. I did get through to her. Somehow or other, in the din, in the misery and humiliation of it all, something or other got heard.

And by the right person: Zuleika.

I'd be glad, if I weren't so damn tired.

Never mind. Thus begins my most amazing day, the day that has everything.

.   .   .

Cindy Fernandez is lecturing me.

I no longer try to argue with Cindy when she lectures me, or hide behind my desk. I have endured, I have come through to the other side and become what I always, truly, was: the quiet yet smart-ass student with the smirk she cannot wipe off her face.

"I hear you were trying to whip up competition, Elizabeth. I hear you were trying to tell 9A to do better than us."

This is true. 9A is my most intellectually gifted class, full of students who would pass if they bothered to pick up a pencil, and they know it. So I've been trying to con them into picking up that pencil. "Hey, kids," I said one day, "let's have a contest. Let's see what class can do the best. I bet you'd win."

Of course they knew they were being conned, but isn't that a pleasure, sometimes, knowing you're being had? If it weren't, seduction wouldn't be a possibility.

"Competition is bad." Cindy waggles her finger at me. "We're not supposed to compete. We're supposed to cooperate. We should all work together. We shouldn't try and be better than anybody. We should all be the same. You were trying to hurt our self-esteem. And that is bad. That is very very bad."


9B is screaming again.

In my attempt to get something, *something*, to grade them on, I have written a few writing topics on the board, but before I can even try to explain, the ululations begin.

Even Peter Garcia has had enough, and I don't blame him. He knows he's passing, with a good grade, and now it's time to relax.

He and Tim'n'Bob and Andrew Santangelo are having a lively talk about skateboarding, and thrilled by this spirit of cooperation, by the sight of no one doing better than anybody else, I am eavesdropping, hoping to learn something.

And then Judy walks in.

Peter and a few others dive for their pens and start to get to work.

"What . . . what's going on?" she says to me.

"We're doing a writing assignment."

"But . . . it's so noisy in here."

"Yeah, I know. Makes concentration kind of difficult."

"Those students on the other side of the room . . . they don't know what's going on."

"I tried to tell them, but no one was listening."

"Aren't you going to go over there and tell them what to do?"

"Why bother?" I say. "They're not going to do it."

"Oh," says Judy, and I smile at her cheerfully, the conversation already slipping from my mind.


But as far as excitement goes, today has hardly begun. This is the day I discover what it's like to be a family. The transformation goes like this:

"What is wrong with you, 9A?" I say. "You know how little *work* it would take to pass this class? Then why don't you do it? Do me a favor. Press the nib of the pen against the paper. Does that hurt? *Move* it, give your hand a little aerobic exercise. Is that so bad? Is it worse than going to summer school?"

"I don't want to go to summer school!" says Vincent.

"You don't?" I say. "You have a funny way of expressing it."

I look 9A over. I don't know why they're listening today, but they are, and suddenly I am inspired. "I tell you what," I say. "Just for a change, do whatever I tell you to do. Okay? For instance . . ." I place my right hand over my left breast and lift my left hand, Pledge of Allegiance style. "Are you ready, class? Do the same. *Now.*"

They do, grinning stupidly.

"Repeat after me," I say. "We, the students of 9A . . ."

"We, the students of 9A . . . ," they rumble back.

"Don't want to go to summer school."

"Don't want to go to summer school."

"Because it is a *drag* to go to summer school."

"Because it is a *drag* to go to summer school."

"A waste of *time* to go to summer school."

"A waste of *time* to go to summer school."

"So we, the students of 9A . . ."

The door creaks open, and I see that Leon has entered the room.

I suppose I should stop, but how can I? I've got momentum here, I've got them perfectly with me, this is our moment, I can't stop.

*In a minute,* I mouth to Leon.

"So we, the students of 9A . . ."

"Are going to work *now.*"

"Are going to work *now.*"

"We will do whatever Elizabeth tells us to do."

"We will do whatever Elizabeth tells us to do."

"We will write whatever Elizabeth tells us to write."

"We will write whatever Elizabeth tells us to write."

"And do a good job."

"And do a good job."

"Because we can."

"Because we can."

"And because we don't want to go to summer school."

"And because we don't want to go to summer school."

"So we are going to pass."

"So we are going to pass."

"Yes, *pass*," I say, and even more inspired, I slowly fold my hand into a fist. "Pass now!"

"Yes, pass. Pass now!"

I pump my fist into the air. "Pass now! Pass now! Pass now!"

"Pass now! Pass now! Pass now!" they repeat, pumping away, and all the while this is happening, Leon stands there, and I don't know what he's thinking: I can't read his face at all.

"Sorry about that," I say. "It's just that we were in the middle of things. What's up?"

"Actually," says Leon, as the class slowly settles down, "I'm here to promote the summer school program. It's going to be a great program this summer, kids! Why, we might even go on a field trip!"

Then he turns to me.

"I'd like to see you in my office, after class," he says.


"Kiss my ass," says Tiffany.

Leon has gone, and I straighten the tables, and say that those students who *still* have no interest in going to summer school might want to do a little bit of writing now, and most of them begin to work. But not Tiffany. She's cut so many classes, she's too far gone for rescue. So she sits, and chats, and I go over to her and say, "Come on, Tiffany, give it a try," and she looks up at me with a superior smile on her face—as if she had been waiting for this since the end of February, as if her contempt for me has finally found the perfect moment—and "Kiss my ass," she says, and I begin to speak.


In the beginning was the Word.

Before there was light, there was a Word.

Before there was water, a *word*.

Before there were vines and trees and ornamental plantings, before crocodiles, and platypi, before rocks, even, before *rocks*, there was a word, the sky—before there *was* a sky—dense with them.

They wait for their vessels, words. They wait hopelessly, and hopefully, for the thing that will give them voice.

In the beginning, and in the end, I imagine, is the word, and standing there, in Room 313, of all places, I look down into Tiffany's face and something breaks in me: something cold, and very hot, like dry ice, it breaks, and a mist comes out of my mouth.

I don't know what I'm saying, for I am that vessel now, and vessels don't take notes.

Everything extraneous—hair, anklebone, thumbnail, my upcoming visit to Leon's office—is burnt away and the only things that remain are mouth, heart, lungs, fury, June, June which is setting me free, but for what, I don't know, I am tired of imagining, but no matter. For these minutes, even imagination is extra. Why imagine when you are utterly in the moment, and the moment is complete? In the beginning was the Word. It needed me, and I needed it, and the only thing I can see is that smug smile dying on Tiffany's face.

And then I am done.

Whatever it is I've said, has been said.

I sag, exhausted, spent.

Silence.

And then, no silence.

Applause.

Yes. Applause.

9A is applauding.

9A is applauding . . . *me.*

All of them: Adam, and Erica, and Eric, and Silvia, and Arden, and Ken, and even Helen, even Mona and Nadia, and Nestor, even Rosalie and Kimberly, and Vincent, Vincent applauding the loudest of all.

Wave after wave, it comes, applause, and I don't know how long it goes on for. I am too far away to either stop them or egg them on. I stand there, breathing hard, saying nothing. I allow them, my subjects, to applaud me.

And then they are done. Tiffany jumps up and runs from the room.

I raise one eyebrow. This is a talent I have always envied in others. Now I seem to possess it, myself.

"Back to work," I say.

. . .

And now I am sitting in Leon's office, with Leon, and Judy, and Calvin, my union representative.

*My union representative?*

"I've heard some serious allegations. Some serious allegations indeed," says Leon.

I look at Calvin, but nothing is given away in that face.

"Judy tells me that she walked into your room this morning and it was very . . . chaotic."

"Well, yeah, that's true," I say, "but . . ."

"She tells me that rather than you trying to do something about it, you were sitting behind your desk, doing nothing."

"Well, yeah, but . . ."

"She tells me that nobody seemed to know what he was supposed to be doing. And that when she came up to you and asked you to explain things, you just said, Why bother? They're all failing anyway."

"Well, not in those exact words . . ."

"This is bad," says Leon. "This is very very bad."

And then I get irritated. "Look," I say. "It's June. School's almost done. I told you I'm not planning to come back. So why are we bothering with this?"

"You know, you've made some progress. I wrote you up a good observation report."

Which, weirdly enough, is true.

"I wish you well, Elizabeth. I was hoping to write you a good recommendation, for wherever you were planning to go in your educational career."

*But I don't want an educational career. When I get out of here, I'm going to write a book and get me a whole bunch of love, sex, fame, and money.*

*And if that doesn't work out, there's another census in 2010, if I can just hold on.*

"And furthermore . . . ," says Leon.

"Yes?"

"Tiffany just came in here and told me that you said to her, quote, 'You can sit in summer school till you rot.'"

So that's what I said. It's good to know.

"Oh?" I say. "And did she tell you that she said to *me*, Kiss my ass?"

Judy and Leon recoil.

"Well," harrumphs Leon, "you're not supposed to stoop to their level."

But I'm not interested in stooping, or not stooping, or anything else Leon has to say. Let him speak. It's all right. Now that I've got at least a line of what I said, I can play back, perfectly, our little drama in 9A. The vow, and Leon coming in, and Tiffany smiling at me, that smile that told me she thought she could do whatever she liked with me, and the words pouring out of my throat, one perfect word after the other, not too loud, not too soft, my body, no, the whole room, in absolute obeisance to whatever it was I was saying, and then of course, the applause. The wave after wave of applause, and later I will think it is just a little bit horrible, the way they were applauding me for besting one of their own, but that's the way it is, that's what happens in the presence of superior power, and for one minute, one minute anyway, as the applause went on and on and I stood, accepting my due, I finally knew what it was like: I had acquired my authority.

coda
**telling tales out of school**

Fire drill!

I didn't know the school had bells, but it turns out that for this we're not going to rely on intuition.

Now that school is all but over, we're having fire drills almost every day. Someone's explained it to me like this: there's a standard number we're supposed to have, and all through the year, we didn't seem to have any, so we're cramming them all in now.

I don't mind. The weather is gorgeous, a walk is always nice, and besides, it might not be a drill at all; it might be a real fire, and with real fires come real firemen.

"Hey," I say to Miriam, as our classes stream out together, "how are you?"

"School's almost over," she says. "Kids? Two rows, please?"

Out the school we march. "Keep going," shouts Tom, "up the sidewalk, make room for the classes behind you."

"There's something I've been meaning to ask you," I say to Miriam. "How does this school compare to other schools?"

She gives an eloquent sidelong glance. "It's weird."

"What do you mean, weird? Do you mean, like bad? Is it worse than other schools?"

"I didn't say worse, and I didn't say better. I said, weirder."

"Weird, how?"

"Weird. Just weird, Elizabeth. Really weird." And she laughs.

Try to worm anything interesting out of a teacher of economics.

"Miriam? Elizabeth? Fire drill. Quiet, please," says Tom.

"Weird in what way?" I whisper to Miriam.

"Okay," says Tom. "Back to class."

The kids begin shuffling, and as they do, an old man somehow slips into the middle of the group. I mean *old*. I mean eighty if he's a day.

He's a good-looking old guy. Shining white hair, skin tanned to dark wood, muscular if somewhat bowed legs emerging from his shorts. A vigorous old guy. He falls perfectly into place and starts to march, swinging his arms as if reliving some old army fantasy.

"Who is he?" whispers Miriam. "A *student?*"

"Yeah. That's right. He's the oldest student at the School of the New Millennium."

"Well, he's certainly good at fire drills," she says. "I guess he's had practice."

"Yes," I whisper. "We're proud of him. So it took him a little bit longer to graduate high school. Some of us just learn differently. There's no shame in that. And now he's ready to graduate! For five minutes, he's going to be a Leader of Tomorrow."

"Miriam? Elizabeth? Quiet," says Tom.


Class is over, and Regents exams have begun. No more peace, love, and understanding: we teachers have been drafted into handing out the pencils, reading out the instructions, announcing *begin* and *stop,* giving permission when students need to go to the bathroom.

Finally I have found work I am suited for.

My favorite task is hall duty. It consists of sitting in the hall—and you know how much I love the hall—and waving the bathroom goers along, one at a time, sometimes throwing in a "Keep it quiet" for sound effects.

Hall duty: a time for idle hanging out, for the dreaming of daydreams, the eating of fried foods, the reading of horoscopes, and of course, the discussing, with one's colleagues, of issues in education.

For instance:

Topic: 2

Boys have it harder then girls today. Boys dont get respect. Girls get longer hair and make more money.

Girls have good looks unlike guys not that I have been looking. Guys will do anything for there girl. I know a guy who bougt a car for his girl. I know guys who will get tatoos of the names of there girls on there gets or backs, arms, legs, stumeks.

I know one guy he got a ratoo of his girl Brandi and then when she went off with another guy he goujed the tatoo off with a knife even though we all said it wasnt worth it. I know another guy who tried to save a girl who was being beat by a old boyfriend. The boyfreiend shot the guy in the head and then when he laid in a pool of blood dying she went off with the old boyfriend the police never solved the crime

"Whaddya think?" I say. "An A? A B? A C?"

"An A, of course. He gets his point across."

"It's so depressing. How come no man ever got a tattoo on his stomach for me?"

"Whaddya think, Park Sang? Would you get a tattoo on your stomach for a girl?"

"Not just any girl. But for the right girl . . . sure."

"Here. Let me have a copy," says Martin, reaching over to pick one up; I have made xeroxes for everybody. "This is the part I like," he says, beginning to read: "Girls have good looks unlike guys *not* that I have been looking. . . ."

As we're busy laughing, Leon walks into the hall.

"Elizabeth? Could I speak to you, please?"

"*Oohh.*" I sigh, under my breath, standing up, hoping no one hears me, or perhaps hoping someone will: "It's *Dad.*"

"Yes?"

"These grades," Leon says. "They're terrible."

"I know they are. But I passed anyone I could. I really did."

"But these *grades.* We can't have so many failing students. Half the class?"

"Not quite. And anyway, those are generous. Surely you know that. These are students who are failing everything else. And furthermore, have been failing all year. There are no surprises here."

"Did you call the parents?" Leon asks. "Did you call each and every one? Did you sit there and explain, did you send follow-up letters, did you call meetings?"

I *had* called some. But calling parents is a full-time job, and after a few exhausting phone conversations, I just gave up.

What can I say? I guess *I* was the one who failed the ninth grade.

"*No,*" I whisper.

"Well. Do something about these grades," Leon says sternly. "When little Johnny comes home with these grades, Mommy and Daddy are going to be very upset. And when Mommy and Daddy are upset, they're going to call me. This school has to survive, Elizabeth."

"Leon told me to fiddle my grades," I announce to the group at large.

Rachel, the furious idealist, says, "How dare he! This is an outrage! How can we call this education?"

Miriam, the cool one who never loses her head, asks if I've kept good records of everything. "That's what I do," she says. "Then I can point to what's not been done. No arguments there."

Park Sang, the cynic, says, "It's not surprising, is it? You're just the first. He's going to take all of us into his office, just you wait. He has to. If everyone fails, we'll lose our charter. So do what he says. I will. Why trouble yourself?"

And Martin, the helpful monk, provider of refuge and magic elixirs, actually comes up with something that makes sense. "Just give the failing ones incompletes instead," he says. "Assign them some work to do this summer, and give them a deadline, and then, if they don't do it, they can fail. What do you think?"

"Who's going to check the work? I'm not going to be here."

"I'll do it. Don't worry, it won't be that much."

And that's the solution I present to Leon. I stand there in his office, waiting for him to veto it.

"That's a good idea. A very good idea," he says. Then he smiles.

It's a funny smile. A sad smile; a wistful smile. A smile that tells me he is perfectly aware of what's going on, and he doesn't know what to do about it. A smile that tells me that he, too, might have avoided spending his nights chasing down parents for discussion after discussion simply so he could have a little peace.

God, I think, it must be awful for him.

Leon loves this school. It is his baby, his dream. Every time he goes to a conference or reads about some new educational theory *which of course is right, no doubt about it, this is the answer to the questions we don't even know how to ask,* he runs back and tries to finagle us into trying it. The school in his head is a beautiful well-run place filled with happy academic achievers and of course, love. And now Tom is leaving, and Nkruma, and the results of the eighth-grade citywide exams are in, and our students did no better than average—no worse, but no better—about two-thirds of them, more or less, reading and writing and doing math below grade level.

I shrug, a little sheepishly. *Sorry, Leon.*

You wanted to hire a saintly believer, and you got me.


I am proctoring three girls taking a make-up exam when Nkruma knocks on the door.

"What's up?" I whisper.

"There's an intruder in the building," he says. "Listen carefully. This is what you have to do. Stand up, go to a corner away from the window, where you can't be seen from the hall. Be very quiet. I'm going to turn off the lights and lock the door from the outside, okay? No need to panic. We just have to check this out."

"Girls?" I say. "Let's go."

In the soft dark of our corner, we huddle together silently.

*This is how Columbine happened.*

You come to school, and it is an ordinary day, even a boring day. And suddenly a door opens, and it becomes the most interesting, and the most terrible, day of your life. Just like that.

I'm telling myself not to be ridiculous. This is some pizza delivery man with the wrong address, or the old guy from the fire drill line, dreaming some old school dream, this is the fireman who's finally come back for me, this is nothing at all.

It's nothing, of course it's nothing.

But nobody says a word.

*Oh my God*, I think, *I'm going to die in this fucking school. I'm going to die.*

*Now that would be the icing on the cake.*

And suddenly it goes: all that seismic rumble and complaint between the generations. It seems so stupid now. Say if you like that we are black or Latino or white or gay or straight or rich or poor, or young or not so young, it doesn't matter. For we *are* in this together. We *are*. And for these minutes, I *love* the girls. Yes, Leon, I truly do. Without reservations. I love their pretty teenaged skin and their pretty teenaged bodies and their taste for Britney Spears and Ricky Martin, why not? Enjoy what you enjoy, girls. Let us breathe together a little bit. Let us simply breathe.

"Since we're standing here," I whisper, "we might as well be introduced."

Now Calvin is unlocking the door, and turning on the lights.

"Drill over," he says. "You can start taking the test again."

"Drill?" I ask.

"Oh yeah," says one of the girls. "We started doing them last year, after Columbine."

"Can't be too careful," says Calvin. "You never know."

And you never do know, I guess, but still: as usual I had been the only one who didn't have a clue about what was supposed to be going on.

Oh well. False alarm.

This time, anyway, it was a false alarm.

Things being what they are, only a moment separates our rescues from our surrender. The exam gets done, the pencils put down, the results are in, and then forgotten. Days go by, and then other days, and Vincent Daly, like those before him, will probably change his mind about dying young and pretty. Old and ugly will suddenly acquire strange attractions.

Yes. One day, and sooner than I would like to think, Vincent will find himself, 205 years old, slumping on the sofa in the subatomic nursing home, playing with the remote. *God, it makes him sick. All those young lovers on the screen. Sashaying around as if they invented it. Hah. He could show them what it was like, he really could, before those goddamn Venusians moved in and ruined everything.*

And the doors will swing open, and here's Erica Reynolds and Eric Antonelli, together, as they've always been, for how can I bear to separate them? "Hi," Vincent will say, and it will all come back to him, taking him like a sudden attack of heartburn: that time when they were ridiculously young together.

"Hey," he'll say. "Remember that weird teacher we had in ninth-grade English? The one who cried, the one who sang, the one who danced the jitterbug in the front of class, the one who fell to her knees and prayed to God, the one who said *fuck*, the one who quoted . . . *poetry*. What do you think happened to her?"

Well, I survived, all limbs intact, and I learned a thing or two in the process.

First—isn't this always the way?—I learned what I knew already: I wasn't born to be a high-school teacher. Anyone who has as much trouble as I do slipping pieces of paper into their appropriate folders should avoid any job that requires keeping order.

Second, I learned that being a teacher is tough. I knew that, too, but until I entered Room 313, with all my book knowledge and fairly good intentions, I had no idea how tough it could be.

I learned about Britney Spears. I can't remember which 9B students insisted on it, but I'm with them: I *know* those are implants.

Sometimes people ask me if I know what has happened to my students. Truthfully, I don't. I've never seen any of them again, so I can only assume that some went on to tenth grade and some had their names permanently engraved on the backs of the chairs in Room 313. Most will go on to live ordinary lives, and some terrible, and perhaps one or two will go on to glory. And not necessarily the ones I expect, either. Despite all our efforts to control experience, to prescribe this or that drug, attend this or that workshop, the way we make—and are made by—our lives remains a mystery.

I've never seen any of the teachers again, either.

Actually, that's not quite true. I once ran into the drama teacher of the School of the New Millennium in a bookstore. I was on the down escalator and she on the up, and as our paths crossed, I greeted her cheerfully. She pretended she hadn't seen me and started walking up her escalator as fast as possible.

I guess she thought students screaming "I hate you!" might be catching.

As I write this, in the summer of 2002, the results of the fourth- and eighth-grade statewide reading exams are in.

After all the hoopla, the talk of raised standards and the speeches of how we must leave no child behind, the children have provided a different answer. In 1999, 35.5 percent of New York City eighth-graders were reading at grade level or above. In 2002, that number fell to 29.5 percent. In other New York State cities— Rochester, Yonkers, Syracuse, Buffalo—the results were even worse, falling from 26.8 percent to 19.3 percent. In fact, the only place where grades improved was in the affluent suburbs. Even with this improvement, the percentage of grade-level readers in the whole state went down—from 48.1 percent to 44.9 percent in 2002.

The politicians were shocked, shocked. Something must be done.

It all seemed so silly to me. Anyone working in a school knows that transformation, despite demands, does not occur overnight. Furthermore, testing is not gospel. Tests are made by human beings, and the kind of human beings who spend their lives designing tests are probably very flawed indeed. But most important, it is foolish to criticize a school system as an entity separate from the society that made it.

Schools don't exist separately from our culture. They *are* our culture. They reflect what we value, disdain, honor, ignore. The *madrasa* belongs to one world. And the American school—be it public or private, urban or suburban or rural—belongs to us, and tells our stories. Our secrets, if you will.

If you think there is a big divide between how our richest and poorest children are educated—and there is—don't blame the schools. Blame the divide. Though actually I hate that word blame. Blame is for sissies, those who want easy targets, and any targets but themselves. Let's simply say, then, consider the divide, all the causes you can come up with, and all the consequences. Schools might be responsible for many things, but they're not responsible for the growing gap between the rich and poor in this country, and what that might mean. And yet you never hear a politician stand up and denounce a world where so many people make so little and CEOs so obscenely much.

One of the reasons schools fail is because school as an institution is the *one* public place where that gap is addressed. Not, by the way, that all problems stem from poverty. Middle-class and wealthy kids have problems, too. They fail classes, take drugs, drive while drunk, kill themselves, or each other. Despair is an equal opportunity employer.

But in places where there's more money, there are armies of private this and private that to bear the burden of what has become the schools' job of social engineering. Now social engineering—instruction on brushing your teeth and raising your hand and waiting for a pass to go to the bathroom—was always part of school. But as our country has become more developed, the demands for that engineering have also become more developed, too. Public schools in less affluent neighborhoods are expected to perform that task as well as wealthy schools, and they have a lot more to do with a lot fewer resources. The result? As Nkruma once told me, "Ninety percent of what I do is social work anyway." He was right.

All too often, this is what school is about: feeding poor kids breakfast and lunch and looking out for signs of sexual abuse. Testing kids when it seems there is something *wrong* with them, not only educationally, but psychologically. Setting up coat funds when the parents are too poor, or too negligent, to buy coats for their kids themselves. School is about drug counseling and contraceptive counseling and anti-tobacco and alcohol counseling. It's about trying to give kids from troubled families or foster care or homeless shelters an alternative. No wonder providing intellectual instruction gets lost in the shuffle. There is only so much space, so much time, so much money. Meanwhile, the discussion about what school should actually be for and what students should learn is often muddled and confused.

Some educators don't even seem to think it matters. As Leon said to me: "You are not teaching a subject. You are teaching children."

I understand the temptation to ignore this part of the discussion. It's hard. For the more uniform a group is in its culture and beliefs, the less controversy there is about what to learn, and the easier it is to teach it. But of course, our country is not uniform. Once you get past the differences of class and race, you must consider what I think is probably the most divisive difference of all: geography. So who are we, anyway? What do we want our students to become?

Usually the battle over what American students should learn is described in conservative versus liberal terms. On one side are those promoting a curriculum that celebrates the values of love of God, country, family, capitalism, reading, writing, and arithmetic. On the other are those who think we should produce sensitive, secular, multicultural, and if white, a little bit guilty for it, citizens of the new global technological universe. The only place where these two sides agree is that all students should then march off to college where they will learn the skills to go make their fortunes. That is, after all, the American dream.

For me, however, dividing educational theory along left/right lines is a false dichotomy. It is so much more complicated than that. And where, in either curriculum, is there a place for those free and interesting and creative discussions?

Far be it from me to fight the culture war. I am, in case you haven't noticed by now, no general.

Besides, there are so many culture wars. Each battle fought in the classroom reflects a larger one fought, either overtly or covertly, in the world outside.

The transformation of our economy from a frontier-based one into an industrial one to a post-industrial one based on knowledge has had vast cultural complications. In the nineteenth century, teenage boys never had to ask themselves if they were of use. They knew they were: doing their apprenticeships, working, and making things. Maybe it was a hard life—I don't want to romanticize this—but those boys had effect. Their work mattered. And through much of the twentieth century, it was still possible for someone who wasn't good at school to have hope for a viable future. If he could manage to graduate from high school, even vocational school, he could go out and get a decent job with middle-class benefits—medical care, vacation, pension.

Not now. *We will leave no child behind.* A sweet thing to say, but I don't believe it for a minute. Some people always get left behind. Once it was African-Americans, who saw doors of opportunity shut to them. And girls, of course, who were told they should study simply for their Mrs. degree. But now it's children whose abilities may lie more in their hands or their hearts or yes, particular crevices of their minds, than in the small spectrum of academic skills that school enshrines.

I sometimes think that the epidemic of learning disabilities currently sweeping our schools is not an epidemic at all. It is instead an attempt to provide a scientific explanation for what is really a cultural disease. There are, of course, kids who do have learning disorders—I have met them. But in a lot of cases, there are kids who simply have talents that our world has no place for. Rather than thinking why that might be, and if there is anything that could be done about it, we try to manipulate kids into self-transformation. They respond by making themselves miserable, and everyone around them, too.

There are other cultural shifts reflected in our schools as well. The confusion, for instance, over what it means to have individual rights and what happens when those individual rights conflict with the rights of others. Call this struggle The Burger King War: sometimes it seems to me that *everybody* wants to have it exactly his way.

There is such a thing as civic good. You see it when you walk through a place like Central Park, or into a public library, or take a subway; you practice it when you give a pregnant woman on a bus your seat, or when you pull to the side of the road so an ambulance might pass. This sense of public space and public behavior is the core of individual rights. For talk about individual rights if you will—I'm for them. But if there is no sense of group good, you can't have individual rights, for then the well-connected, the vociferous, and the selfish will be so intent on having their rights that you won't be able to have any.

While I won't take the School of the New Millennium as a paradigm, I suspect that its struggle to please all parties, to offend no one, because someone might start griping about his rights, is reflected in textbooks and in schools all over the country. The result is mediocrity. As for its demand that its teachers and better-behaved students practice saintly understanding—the result is insanity. Try to possess for five minutes the kind of moral control and tolerance demanded of students like Peter Garcia, and Sarah, and Arden, and Adam, and Silvia, and Erica, and Eric Antonelli, and you'll know what I mean.

I have not even begun to talk about the American confusion about the intellectual life, and how that confusion has been exacerbated by our adoration of new technology and the computer, which is seen not as a tool, but, somehow, as a cure. Now don't get me wrong, computer knowledge is a useful and practical thing to possess. But to replace the culture of the book—the concept that anything worth learning is both difficult and time-consuming, but pays the learner back with all kinds of contradictory pleasures—with the concept that in our busy, multitasking world, knowledge is something that should be broken down into easily digested nuggets and "skills" is a mistake. Efficient such a way of learning might be. Better it is not. And if you don't believe me, check our country's reading scores. The more guaranteed-to-work computers and magic programs they drag in the worse a lot of students do.

As for me, I believe not in "reading skills," but in literature. I believe not in reading scores, but in thought and understanding. I believe, I guess, in "free and interesting and creative discussions." Let Cindy Fernandez announce what the rules of the world are, and how she was the one who knew them. Let Leon pander to her. But Peter and Adam have a bigger world in mind. They *read*. They have already encountered hundreds of voices, voices much more eloquent than Cindy's could ever be. If you don't encounter those voices, how will you ever know how small your corner of the universe really is, and how great are the possibilities beyond it?

I wonder what will happen to those boys. Good things, I hope.

But that, class, is another book. A book that somebody else—maybe even Peter or Adam—should write. As for me, even though there's no clock on the wall, and no bells either, and we're months away from the next summer vacation, I think it's finally time I graduated from high school.

## acknowledgments

I am indebted to the Corporation of Yaddo, the Virginia Center for the Creative Arts, and the Writers Room in New York City, as well as to Darcy Bacon of National Public Radio, for all her encouragement and the chance to sit in that really cool recording booth wearing the cool headphones.

Thank you to Susan Bargman, Laura Goldman, Belle Waring, and Beth Wolfson, the first readers of this manuscript, and who, along with Nancy Brokaw, Jamie Callan, Ben Gibberd, Alison Jarvis, Roberta Lawrence, Mary Ann Newman, Sheila Phalon, Joe Razza, Deborah Thielker, and Penny Wolfson, provided me with conversation, patience with my trials and tribulations, laughs, and spiritual first aid.

My gratitude to my family, with an extra gold star to Andrew, for riding in on his white horse when that's what was needed.

I thank Janice Eidus, for her invaluable advice; Cheryl Pientka, who pulled an early version of this manuscript out of the slush pile; my agent, Henry Dunow, and Ashley Shelby of Tarcher/Putnam.

Along with some of my more terrifying encounters, I met some pretty wonderful people—teachers, staff, parents, and students—at the School of the New Millennium. Some of the latter may even become Leaders of Tomorrow. I'm looking forward to seeing that.

And finally, in memory of Qunzelle Hope: The world's a dimmer place without you, Girl.

about the author

Elizabeth Gold has written for *Salon*, *The Washington Post*, and such literary journals as *Field*, *The Indiana Review*, and *Mid-American Review*. She lives in New York City.